SN-7
3/05

FERGUSON
CAREER BIOGRAPHIES

CONDOLEEZZA
RICE

National Security Advisor and Musician

Bernard Ryan, Jr.

Ferguson

An imprint of ☑ Facts On File

Condoleezza Rice: National Security Advisor and Musician

Ferguson
An imprint of Facts On File, Inc.
132 West 31st Street
New York NY 10001

Ryan, Bernard, 1923–
    Condoleeza Rice. national security advisor and musician / Bernard Ryan, Jr.
        p. cm.
Includes index.
Summary: A biography of Condoleeza Rice, known both and as an accomplished pianist and for serving as George W. Bush's National Security Advisor.
    ISBN 0-8160-5480-0 (hc: alk. paper)
    1. Rice, Condoleezza, 1954—Juvenile literature. 2. National Security Council (U.S.)—Biography—Juvenile literature. 3. Presidents—United States—Staff—Biography—Juvenile literature. [1. Rice, Condoleezza, 1954- . 2. National Security Council (U.S.)–Biography. 3. Women–Biography. 4. African Americans–Biography.] I. Title.

UA23.15.R93 2004
355'.033073'092—dc22   2003015340

Ferguson books are available at special discounts when purchased in bulk quantities for businesses, associations, institutions, or sales promotions. Please call our Special Sales Department in New York at (212) 967-8800 or (800) 322-8755.

You can find Ferguson on the World Wide Web at http://www.fergpubco.com

Text design by David Strelecky

Pages 97–146 adapted from Ferguson's *Encyclopedia of Careers and Vocational Guidance, Twelfth Edition*

Printed in the United States of America

MP FOF 10 9 8 7 6 5 4 3 2 1

This book is printed on acid-free paper.

CONTENTS

"RAISED ...
TO BE A LADY"

On Monday, April 23, 2002, the audience at the Kennedy Center in Washington, D.C., rose to its feet, offering a standing ovation. Its enthusiastic applause saluted cellist Yo-Yo Ma and the smiling woman at the piano who had just accompanied him. She was not only an accomplished pianist. She was also President George W. Bush's national security advisor, Condoleezza Rice.

Born November 14, 1954, in Birmingham, Alabama, Condoleezza Rice was named by her mother after the Italian musical direction *con dolcezza*, which means "with sweetness." She first began taking piano lessons when she was three years old. At that age, she had already learned to read, and soon she took up figure skating, ballet dancing, and the French language.

Condoleezza's mother, Angelena, taught music and science at an all-black high school. Her father, John

Cellist Yo-Yo Ma and Condoleezza Rice perform at the Kennedy Center in Washington, D.C., 2002. (Getty Images)

Wesley Rice, was pastor at Birmingham's Westminster Presbyterian Church and also a high school guidance counselor. Both parents believed strongly in the value of education and encouraged their precocious daughter, who was their only child, to learn quickly and well.

After only a year of piano lessons, four-year-old Condoleezza gave her first "public" performance. It was at a tea welcoming new teachers in the Birmingham school system. Wearing a taffeta dress and a fuzzy-looking tamo'-shanter hat, she played a piece that was adapted from a longer work by Tchaikovsky. It was called "A Doll's Funeral." For the next several years she played occasionally at a number of public events.

The atmosphere of Condoleezza's upbringing encouraged her to believe that anything is possible if you put your mind—and your best efforts—to it. Years later Condoleezza said that her parents often assured her she could become president of the United States if she wanted. When her father took her to visit Washington, D.C., when she was eight years old, she gazed at the White House and said, "One day, I'll be in that house."

By the time she was 10, Condoleezza felt she had had enough of the piano. She told her mother she wanted to quit playing. "You're not old enough or good enough to make that decision," said her mother. "When you are old enough and good enough, then you can quit, but not now."

Condoleezza skipped two grades, reaching eighth grade at age 11. Her parents were extremely proud of their daughter's achievements, and they believed that her education and intelligence would help her overcome some of the disadvantages that African-Americans faced at the time. "My parents were very strategic," she said years later. "I was going to be so well prepared, and I was going to do all of these things that were revered in white society so well, that I would be armored somehow from racism. I would be able to confront white society on its own terms."

Birmingham in the 1960s

The Rice home was in Titusville, a middle-class but segregated section of Birmingham. The city during Condoleezza's childhood was a world of racism. Water fountains and rest room doors bore signs saying COLORED ONLY or WHITE ONLY. In 1961, when Condoleezza was seven, she was shopping in a Birmingham department store with her mother. She found a pretty dress that she wanted to try on, but a white saleswoman blocked her from entering a fitting room reserved for white customers. The saleswoman directed Condoleezza and her mother to a storage room used by blacks.

Mrs. Rice calmly told the saleswoman they would use the fitting room or she would take her business—and the commission the saleswoman expected to earn—to another store. The saleswoman relented, but stood at the door hoping no one would notice. Condoleezza still remembers the experience, and years later General Colin Powell commented, "Condi was raised first and foremost to be a lady. She was raised in a protected environment to be a person of great self-confidence in Birmingham, where there was no reason to have self-confidence because you were a 10th-class citizen and you were black."

The civil rights movement brought much fighting to Birmingham. In May 1963, its police challenged demonstrators, many of whom were children, by turning vicious dogs and powerful fire hoses on them. "My parents really provided a shield as much as they could against the horrors of Birmingham," Condoleezza recalls. "At the same time I can remember my parents taking me to watch the ➤

The 1963 bombing of Birmingham's 16th Street Baptist Church took the life of one of Condoleezza's friends. (© Photo by the *Birmingham News,* 2003. All rights reserved. Reprinted with permission.)

marchers—they wanted us to know the history and to know what was happening."

In September 1963, when Condoleezza was nine, a blast of dynamite rocked Birmingham's 16th Street Baptist Church, killing four little girls. "The bombing was meant to suck hope out of the future," Condoleezza said years later, "by showing that hope could be killed—child by child. My neighborhood friend, Denise McNair, was killed in that bombing, and though I didn't see it, I heard it a few blocks away. And it is a sound that I can still hear today."

Deeply Religious Family

Like education, religion was an important part of daily life in Condoleezza Rice's family. She often speaks of her Granddaddy Rice, who grew up as a poor farmer's son in Ewtah, Alabama. "One day," she says, "he decided he needed to get book-learning. And so he asked, in the language of the day, where a colored man could go to school. They said a little Presbyterian school, about 50 miles away, named Stillman College. So he saved up his cotton to pay for his first year's tuition and he took off for Tuscaloosa. After the first year, he ran out of cotton and he needed a way to pay his tuition. My grandfather asked the school administrators how those other boys were staying in school, and he was told that they had what was called a scholarship. And if he wanted to be a Presbyterian minister, then he could have a scholarship, too. My grandfather said, 'You know, that's exactly what I had in mind.' And my family has been Presbyterian and college educated ever since. What my grandfather understood, and what I experienced years later, is the transforming power of education."

Thus, in addition to the power of education, Condoleezza was taught to believe in the power of faith. For example, while visiting her grandmother's home when she was 12, Condoleezza saw her Uncle Alto become seriously ill. Her parents and other relatives were excitedly trying to get him to the hospital, but her grandmother was sitting quietly with her arms folded. Condoleezza asked, "Grandmother, aren't you worried about Alto?" Her grandmother answered, "God's will be done." The event convinced Condoleezza that in a crisis God was in control.

Inspiration and New Interests

In 1965 John Rice moved from his high school job to become dean of students at Stillman College. Two years later he was invited to become assistant director of admissions at the University of Denver, where he had taken summertime graduate courses. He also taught a course called "Black Experience in America."

As a young teenager, Condoleezza sat in on some of her father's classes. She was especially impressed by one class, in which a woman named Fannie Lou Hamer was a guest speaker.

Mrs. Hamer gave the students a powerful message. She told them how she had grown up as a child of sharecroppers in Mississippi (sharecropping was a system of farming in which workers could live on a plantation if they cultivated the land and shared the profits from the crop with the plantation owner). At age 12, she had dropped out of school after sixth grade to help support her family by working in the fields.

In 1962 when she was 35 years old, Fannie Lou Hamer joined 17 other African-Americans who rode a bus to their county courthouse to register to vote. They were arrested and jailed by police who said their bus was the wrong color. Released and back home, Fannie Lou Hamer was told by her plantation owner that she would have to get off his land if she insisted on voting. She moved out the same day.

Over the next year Fannie Lou worked on voter registration programs for the Southern Christian Leadership Conference and the Student Nonviolent Coordinating Committee. With others, she endured being arrested and jailed, as well as severe beatings. Then in 1964, a national election year, she was part of a delegation from the Mississippi Freedom Democratic Party (MFDP) that went to the national Democratic party convention in Atlantic

Fannie Lou Hamer, one of Condoleezza's role models, speaks at the Democratic National Convention, 1964. (Associated Press)

City, New Jersey. There the Democratic candidate for president was to be nominated. The convention's delegates from Mississippi, however, were all white people.

Fannie Lou Hamer appeared before the Credentials Committee of the convention. (The committee's purpose was to decide who was authorized to participate in the convention.) She challenged the admission of the all-white delegation from Mississippi because, since most black people were not allowed to vote, it did not fairly represent all the people of their state.

The television networks broadcast Fannie Lou Hamer's testimony to the committee nationwide, including her unforgettable words, "I'm sick and tired of being sick and tired." Now the Democrats gave voting and speaking rights in the convention to two delegates from the MFDP and seated the others as honored guests. They also agreed that in the future they would not seat anyone from a state where citizens were illegally denied the right to vote. A year later President Lyndon B. Johnson signed the Voting Rights Act. It gave federal registrars the power to register African-American voters in every state.

Fannie Lou Hamer went on to become a popular speaker at meetings nationwide. The next year *Mississippi* magazine named her one of six "Women of Influence" in the state. She soon founded the Freedom Farm Cooperative, enabling some 5,000 people to own land and grow their own food.

Condoleezza never forgot Fannie Lou Hamer's visit to her father's classroom. Many years later she was to say, "Ms. Hamer reminds us that heroes are not born, they are made. And they often come from unlikely places. History teaches that it takes just a single, determined individual to bring profound change."

In 1970 after graduating from high school in Denver at age 15, Condoleezza entered the University of Denver. By that time, she was an accomplished pianist and intended to major in music. In her sophomore year, however, she took a course given by Josef Korbel, professor of international studies. He was the father of future U.S. Secretary of State Madeleine Albright. "He gave a lecture on Josef Stalin," Condoleezza later recalled, "and the politics was so Byzantine, there was so much intrigue, I decided I wanted to study the Soviet Union."

2

"SAVED ... BY RUSSIA"

As Condoleezza Rice slowly became an expert on the Soviet Union and Eastern Europe, she knew she would not become a professional musician. "I was saved from a music major by Russia," she often says, adding that she realized she would never get to perform in Carnegie Hall by being "just pretty good." The most she could expect, she decided, would be to earn a living "teaching 13-year-olds to murder Beethoven."

Instead, her new calling was "Soviet politics, Soviet everything." As Professor Korbel became her mentor in international politics with a concentration in Soviet studies, it was, she said, "like falling in love. I just suddenly knew that's what I wanted to do."

At the same time as she was falling in love with Soviet studies, Condoleezza was showing her mettle in the classroom. One day William Shockley, a visiting lecturer who

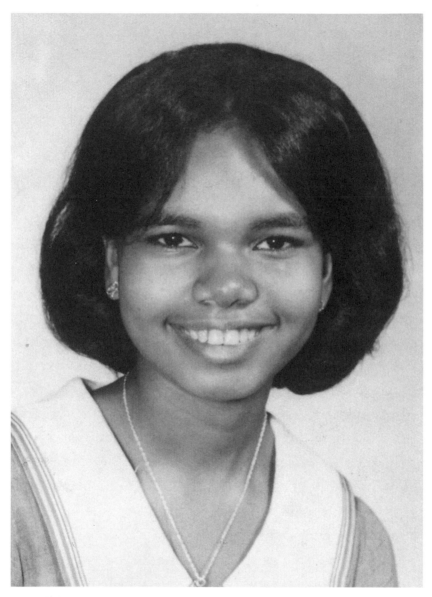

Condoleezza's University of Denver yearbook photo.
(University of Denver)

was famous as one of the inventors of the transistor, expressed his opinion that black people were by nature less intelligent than white people. Condoleezza raised her hand. "You really should not be presenting this as fact," she told him and all who were in the lecture hall, "because there's plenty of evidence to the contrary. Let me explain to you. I speak French. I play Bach. I'm better in your culture than you are."

Honors Grad at Nineteen

When Condoleezza graduated from the University of Denver in 1974 with cum laude honors and a membership in Phi Beta Kappa, she was 19 years old. She was also a competitive ice skater, an accomplished pianist, and an ardent football fan. In fact, while she was a college student, she became engaged to marry a player on the Denver Broncos football team, but they later broke off the engagement.

Now Condoleezza was a young expert on the Soviet and Eastern Europe, but she had no idea what to do with her knowledge. Professor Korbel urged her to continue her studies. Through the benefit of their experiences with education and guidance, her parents directed her to the Department of Government and International Studies at the University of Notre Dame, which had one of the nation's best programs on Soviet history and affairs. There she was advised by a new mentor named George Brinkley, who had been a notable Notre Dame professor since 1958.

Brinkley quickly saw the quality of his young graduate student. "She was extremely bright," he later recalled, "so she came better prepared than most students. She had some Russian before she came to Notre Dame, but my impression was that she learned very quickly and just had a talent. I could see that she was someone who was so highly motivated, and who had also read a tremendous amount."

Her mentor gave her opportunities to work independently, concentrating on military strategy. "Condi developed a very strong interest in the Soviet military," he said, "and in the problems of arms control and Soviet-American relations."

While earning her master's degree, Condoleezza told her friend Professor Korbel that she was thinking about going to law school. "You are very talented," he replied. "You have to become a professor." Condoleezza had such respect and admiration for Korbel, she later said, that she took the idea seriously.

She wanted to be certain about such a plan. So after she received her master of arts degree in government on August 8, 1975, Condoleezza spent the next year taking courses in world affairs at the University of Denver's Graduate School of International Studies (GSIS), a college department Korbel had founded. Then, convinced her future was in college teaching, she enrolled in Korbel's GSIS to earn her Ph.D. in political science.

A New Party and Title

Condoleezza had always considered herself a Democrat. In 1979, however, as a graduate student specializing in the Soviet Union, she was disappointed in the response of U.S. President Jimmy Carter, who was a Democrat, to the Soviet invasion of Afghanistan. Carter said he was simply shocked and saddened, and then stopped U.S. shipments of grain to the Soviets and kept U.S. teams from participating in the 1980 Summer Olympic Games in Moscow. Condoleezza thought the Carter administration showed a weak attitude toward Soviet power. She switched to the Republican Party.

When she was awarded her Ph.D. in 1981 Condoleezza became Dr. Rice. Her life at this time, however, was not focused on political science alone. Other students knew that she continued to teach piano in order to maintain her own technique, that she sang in her church choir, and that she could talk football—*really* talk football—with the most knowledgeable fans.

Professor with Velvet-Glove Forcefulness

Now the 26-year-old Dr. Rice applied to Stanford University in Palo Alto, California, for a fellowship in its Center for International Security and Arms Control. The center's studies concentrated on arms-control agreements with the Soviet Union. Condoleezza became the center's first female fellow, and within a year was invited to join Stanford's political science department as an assistant professor.

One of her fellow teachers, Coit Blacker, recalls meeting her. "I think what struck people at the time," he says, "was a combination of all the personal stuff—charm and very gracious personality . . . a kind of intellectual agility mixed with velvet-glove forcefulness. She's a steel magnolia. She has a wonderful kind of Southern affect in the positive sense—a kind of graciousness. But mixed with this is a very steely inner core. She always knows what she wants and is extremely disciplined, both at personal and professional levels."

Blacker first saw evidence of Condoleezza's "steely inner core" when he happened to be with her one day while she shopped for costume jewelry. When Condoleezza asked about higher priced items, the salesclerk made a demeaning remark. "Let's get one thing straight," said Condoleezza. "You're behind the counter because you have to work for six dollars an hour. I'm on this side asking to see the good jewelry because I make considerably more."

Getting Back to Her Religious Roots

When she first moved to California, Condoleezza was not attending church regularly. As a specialist in international

Smiling for the camera on the University of Denver campus.
(University of Denver)

politics, she often traveled abroad. "I was always in another time zone," she says. But one Sunday she was shopping for spices in a supermarket near her home. An African-American man who was buying supplies for his church picnic turned to her and asked, "Do you play the piano by any chance?"

Condoleezza started playing for the man's Baptist church. "That got me regularly back into church-going," she says. "I don't play gospel very well—I play Brahms—and you know how black ministers will start a song and the musicians will pick it up? I had no idea what I was doing and so I called my mother, who had played for Baptist churches. 'Mother,' I said, 'they just start. How am I supposed to do this?' She said, 'Honey, play in C and they'll come back to you.' And that's true. I thought to myself, 'My goodness, God has a long reach.' I mean, in the Lucky's Supermarket on a Sunday morning."

After playing for the Baptist church for six months, Condoleezza became active with Palo Alto's Menlo Park Presbyterian Church. "I started to go to Bible study," she says, "and to have a more active prayer life. It was a very important turning point in my life."

Personal Loss and Wide Recognition

In 1984, only three years after starting as a teacher at Stanford, Condoleezza won the Walter J. Gore Award for

Excellence in Teaching. Her class had become one of the most popular with undergraduate students. She was busy writing articles on the foreign and defense policies of Soviet and East European countries, and she made speeches to eager audiences. Also in 1984 her first book was published: *The Soviet Union and the Czechoslovak Army, 1948-1983: Uncertain Allegiance.*

In 1985 Condoleezza won the position of national fellow at the Hoover Institution, a so-called "think tank" where some 60 scholars of all ages study and write. The goals of its work are to (1) secure and safeguard peace, (2) improve the human condition, and (3) limit government intrusion into the lives of individuals. Condoleezza was thrilled with the honor since she would be working among some of the best minds in the nation.

However, that same year, the joy of her new position was offset by sadness: Her mother, Angelena Rice, died of breast cancer.

The Hoover fellowship, running from September 1985 to August 1986, gave Condoleezza time to write her second book, titled *The Gorbachev Era.* Her coauthor was Alexander Dallin, director of Stanford's Center for Russian and East European Studies. To write a book with him was an enviable honor for Condoleezza, for Dallin was old enough to be her father. He had published his classic study, *German Rule in Russia, 1941–1945* (a book that is still widely read), when Condoleezza was three years old. In a long career, he had become a well-known expert on Soviet matters.

To Washington and Joint Chiefs of Staff

Condoleezza had kept in touch with her old professor and mentor at Notre Dame, George Brinkley. Now he suggested she apply for an International Affairs Fellowship offered by the Council on Foreign Relations. The Council is a nonpartisan research organization (meaning it is not affiliated with the Democratic or Republican parties) that publishes the magazine *Foreign Policy*. The Council works to improve understanding of the world and to propose ideas on U.S. foreign policy. Its fellowships give scholars and teachers a chance to work in government for a year.

Winning the fellowship put Condoleezza in the Pentagon in the fall of 1986. She was special assistant to the director at the Joint Chiefs of Staff office. The Joint Chiefs include the six commanding officers of the U.S. Military: the chairman and the vice chairman of the Joint Chiefs; the chief of staff, U.S. Army; the chief of naval operations; the chief of staff, U.S. Air Force; and the commandant of the Marine Corps.

It was an extra busy time at the Pentagon, for President Ronald Reagan was building up America's defense systems. Spending for defense grew by 28 percent during his first four years in office.

As she worked under the direction of Admiral William J. Crowe Jr., who was chairman of the Joint Chiefs, Condoleezza's duties included research and planning on U.S. strategy for the use of nuclear arms. "There were four of us in one little office and it was great," she recalls. "I gained so much respect for military officers and what they do, and I think I really got an experience that few civilians have."

3

"TOUGH AS NAILS"

Back at Stanford in 1986 Condoleezza resumed teaching, but she also spent time in community service and accepted invitations to make speeches in far-off places. The Stanford Mid-Peninsula Urban Coalition was doing the kind of work her father had done in Birmingham: helping minorities solve such problems as housing, education, health, and starting businesses. In its Peninsula Academies, the coalition supplied both academic and vocational training for minority students who were likely to drop out of high school. Condoleezza served on the Coalition's board of directors, where she put to use the skills she had learned at the Pentagon about seeing policy made into action.

By now Condoleezza Rice had a wide reputation as a bright young expert on Soviet-American relations. The University of Michigan invited her to spend several days in November 1987 leading a student seminar and speaking about Soviet leader Mikhail Gorbachev at its Center for Russian and East European Studies. In April 1988 the U.S. ambassador to the Union of Soviet Socialist Republics (USSR) invited Condoleezza to speak in Moscow. On May 9 of the next year a nationwide radio audience heard her deliver a speech entitled "U.S.-Soviet Relations: The Gorbachev Era" at a meeting of San Francisco's Commonwealth Club, which had been sponsoring speeches by leaders in public affairs since former President Theodore Roosevelt addressed it in 1911.

In 1987, Stanford's political science department held a dinner at which Condoleezza met a man named Brent Scowcroft. He was a graduate of the United States Military Academy at West Point who spoke fluent Russian and had taught Russian history at the academy. As military aide to President Richard M. Nixon, he had helped to set up the President's historic trips to China and to the Soviet Union.

After the Stanford dinner Scowcroft attended one of Condoleezza's classes and heard her lecture on the MX missile. Condoleezza's detailed understanding of the world's most powerful ICBMs (intercontinental ballistics missiles), each of which contained 10 nuclear warheads that could be aimed individually, impressed Scowcroft.

President George H. Bush and National Security Advisor Brent Scowcroft. (Associated Press)

Special Assistant to the President

Early in 1989 new U.S. President George Herbert Walker Bush named Scowcroft as his national security advisor. Scowcroft called Condoleezza and asked her to take leave from Stanford and bring her fluent Russian and her expertise on Soviet matters to the National Security Council (NSC). At 34 she became the NSC's director of Soviet and Eastern Affairs. Within four months, she was moved up to senior director as well as special assistant to the president for national security affairs.

Scowcroft later said he chose Condoleezza Rice because "she had extensive knowledge of Soviet history and politics, great objective balance in evaluating what was going on, and a penetrating mind with an affinity for strategy and conceptualization. She was charming and affable, but could be tough as nails when the situation required."

On the job Condoleezza had three basic duties. One was to coordinate the work of various assistants who assembled information for the process of making policy. Another was to act as Scowcroft's assistant, writing papers that suggested issues he might raise at top-level meetings and preparing him for the visits of foreign officials. In a third duty, she served as the president's "personal foreign policy staff," writing papers that briefed President Bush on matters to be discussed at meetings with other heads of state.

Condoleezza had been at the NSC for only two months when President Bush, who was thinking about future meetings with Soviet president Gorbachev, asked for a history of U.S. policy toward the USSR. The long report that was produced, called a National Security Review, seemed to Scowcroft to be not only vague but also short on ideas. Scowcroft asked Condoleezza and her team to write a paper that reported in detail on Gorbachev's policies and his ideas for the future.

It was an ideal opportunity for Condoleezza. She had already written widely about Gorbachev, publishing articles in magazines and contributing chapters to books on the Soviet Union. Now she had a chance for the first time to help mold her country's policy toward another world power.

The lengthy memo that she composed became the basis for the policy of the first Bush administration toward the Soviet Union. The memo said that America would do four things: (1) use a clear, confident agenda to strengthen the image of U.S. foreign policy; (2) assure U.S. allies that the U.S. is committed to them and to the control of arms; (3) in Eastern European countries, promote the independence promised them by Gorbachev's reforms; and (4) cooperate with the Soviet Union to "aggressively promote regional stability."

The test of Condoleezza's proposal came in April when Poland, led by its new Solidarity labor union, ended 45 years of communism. By July she was a member of the official team that toured Poland and Hungary with President Bush. As the president delivered speeches Condoleezza had written, he promised crowds that the U.S. supported movements toward democracy in Eastern Europe.

November brought the fall of the Berlin Wall and the reunification of Germany after 45 years as the separate countries of East Germany and West Germany. Now the world began to see the opening of Eastern Europe—Condoleezza's area of greatest expertise—to democracy.

"She tells me everything I know."

December 1989 found Condoleezza aboard the USS *Belknap* with the American Sixth Fleet in Valletta Harbor, Malta, in the Mediterranean Sea. There President Bush was holding the "Malta Summit" meeting with Soviet president Gorbachev. They agreed that the cold war was over. "The arms race, mistrust, psychological, and ideological struggle," said Gorbachev, "all these things should be of the past."

By now Condoleezza was so trusted and respected that no one was surprised to hear how Bush introduced her to Mikhail Gorbachev. "This is Condoleezza Rice," he said. "She tells me everything I know about the Soviet Union." Without hesitation, the Soviet leader told her, "I hope you know a lot."

President George H. Bush (right) has lunch with Soviet President Mikhail Gorbachev (left) during the 1989 Malta Summit. (U.S. National Archives)

Even though Condoleezza had proven herself to be a leading expert on the Soviet Union, she still faced a lot of challenges. "It was initially hard for the Russians to accept me,"

Condoleezza said later. "I never figured out if it was because I was female, or black, or young. But by and large, they've managed to deal with it." She added that she thought the Russians "would sometimes feel, 'What's a girl like you doing here amidst bombs and bullets?'"

Not only did the Russians deal with it, when Gorbachev toured the United States in June 1990 they willingly accepted Condoleezza as the leader of a group of Americans who escorted him to a number of cities. In a letter written later to a journalist, President Bush showed how much he respected her:

> Condi was brilliant, but she never tried to flaunt it while in meetings with foreign leaders. . . . Her temperament was such that she had an amazing way of getting along with people, of making a strong point

without being disagreeable to those who differed. . . . She has a manner and presence that disarms the biggest of the big shots. Why? Because they know she knows what she is talking about.

For Condoleezza, meetings with foreign leaders were becoming almost routine. When European leaders met in Moscow in September 1990 to sign the Treaty on the Final Settlement with Respect to Germany, which brought East and West Germany together at last, she was standing just behind the signers' table.

Now she and Scowcroft talked about the future. He wanted her to stay on the job in Washington. It had been an exciting time, she later said. "You could go to bed one night and wake up with some country having changed its social system overnight, with a new democracy to deal with." But she also said, "I think of myself as an academic first."

"SHE KNOWS A LOT OF PEOPLE"

For almost two years, Condoleezza had been working 14-hour days, often seven days a week. "It's a burnout job," she said. She missed her students and the vigorous mental life they led. She decided to return to Stanford. When she left Washington, D.C., in March 1991, she was 36 years old.

Busy Days for a Busy Mind

Life changed but hardly slowed down for Condoleezza. After die-hard Communists in Moscow tried to throw Gorbachev out, she wrote a major article published in *Time* magazine in September 1991. It concluded that the Soviet army, which had not supported the attempt, could still help find "a stable and democratic successor to the communist Soviet Union. If that is to happen, personnel changes are not enough. A stable democracy needs sturdy institutions, not just charismatic personalities."

Gorbachev himself seemed to enjoy keeping in touch with the young woman who had told President Bush everything he knew about the Soviet Union. During a trip to the western United States before the USSR collapsed, Gorbachev visited Stanford and was escorted on the campus by Condoleezza. Then, not long after he lost power in December 1991, he welcomed a visit from her. With her usual directness, she invited him to contribute his historic papers to the Hoover Institution. With his usual directness, he declined.

Over the next two years Condoleezza not only taught graduate students at Stanford, she again served at the Hoover Institution, this time as a senior fellow. She spoke nationwide by radio on the "End of the Cold War: Challenge for U.S. Policy" from a meeting of the Commonwealth Club. Serving on an advisory panel to California's newly elected Republican governor, Pete Wilson, she proposed recommendations on the reorganization of the state's legislature and of the boundaries of its congressional districts. And she joined her father and his new wife (he had remarried in 1989) to found the Center for a New Generation. This after-school enrichment program gave poor third- to eighth-grade children of the Ravenswood School District in East Palo Alto their first experiences with computers and foreign languages. The program also provided tutoring for them in science and math.

That was not all. In 1991 she served as a television commentator on Soviet affairs for the ABC network. The next year she was a featured speaker at the Republican National Convention in Houston that nominated President Bush for a second term. She also became active in several national groups that studied and made recommendations on American foreign policy, including the Lincoln Club of North Carolina, the American Political Science Association, and the Aspen Strategy Group, where Brent Scowcroft was cochairman. At Stanford she taught in the classroom and advised graduate students. She also served—all in 1991—on three separate search committees that sought a new football coach, a new dean of admissions, and a new university president. In Condoleezza Rice's life there was, as the old saying goes, never a dull moment.

The Oil Tanker *Condoleezza Rice*

Condoleezza had just returned to Stanford from her White House service when the Chevron Corporation invited her to join its board of directors. A worldwide operator, Chevron bought, sold, and produced oil and oil products in 25 countries on six continents. With major interests in Kazakhstan oil, located in part of the former Soviet Union, it welcomed Condoleezza's knowledge of the area. She participated in the planning for Chevron's construction of a pipeline across southern Russia from the Tengiz oil field to a port on the Black Sea.

The value of Condoleezza's background and skills to a company like Chevron was explained by a Texas A&M University professor of management, Albert A. Cannella Jr., who studied how people get on corporate boards. "She knows a lot of people in government," he said, "and that's something a corporation is always looking for. In particular, those with a background in government service are in demand on boards of industries where there is a lot of government regulation and oversight."

The work on Chevron's board was a good fit with Condoleezza's experience and interests. She chaired its public policy committee, taking responsibility for perceiving political, social, and environmental issues that the company should address wherever it did business. She was paid $35,000 each year, plus $1,500 each time she attended a committee meeting or board meeting. Over the next 10 years, she accumulated more than 3,000 shares of Chevron stock, valued at some $241,000.

In 1993 Chevron asked Condoleezza to fly to Rio de Janeiro, Brazil, for the launching ceremony for one of its new 136,000-ton supertankers. At Chevron's insistence, as she smashed the bottle of champagne against the ship's bow, she christened it the *Condoleezza Rice*.

Director, Trustee, Professor, Provost

The honors and the demands on Condoleezza's time and energy continued as other giant corporations followed Chevron's lead. In 1991 the mammoth insurance, financial, and real estate company Transamerica made her a company director. So did computer colossus Hewlett-Packard. That same year her musical soul welcomed positions on the board of governors of the San Francisco Symphony and on the board of trustees of the National Endowment for the Humanities, which makes grants to students and to cultural organizations. Soon she was also a director of the RAND Corporation, a research group that, years earlier, originated the term "think tank."

May 1993 brought an honor from Stanford. Condoleezza Rice was promoted to a full professorship, a recognition seldom given to a 38-year-old teacher in a major university. A month later she was called to the office of Stanford's president, Gerhard Casper. The president looked at her and came right to the point. "Condi," he said, "I want you to be the next provost."

The provost of a university is its chief operating officer, second only to its president. The provost is responsible for making the place work. In the job that Condoleezza was offered, she would have to handle an annual budget of $1.5 billion. The budget at that time included a deficit of $20 million, which meant that every year the college spent $20 million more than it took in. In addition the school would soon be facing an expense of $200 million for repairs under way on some 200 buildings damaged by the 1989 earthquake in the San Francisco Bay Area. The position was really two jobs in one: The provost also served as the university's chief academic officer, making decisions involving 1,400 teachers, 14,000 students, and their entire curriculum.

Condoleezza welcomed the challenges of this position and said yes to the offer. In September 1993 she took office as provost of Stanford University.

5

"YOU HAVE TO MAKE DIFFICULT DECISIONS"

Stanford provosts had always been men, and none of them African-American. All had been some 20 years older than the bright, tough-as-nails but amiable, 38-year-old Condoleezza Rice. All the previous provosts had come up through the ranks, serving as a department chairman, then as a dean. So many people at Stanford questioned the appointment of the young professor who had no such experience. Yet the provost who was retiring, Gerald Lieberman, had the same confidence in Condoleezza that Stanford's president had. "She has tremendous ability and intelligence," said Lieberman when she was appointed, "and the maturity of someone far beyond her age."

Then, too, Condoleezza was a Republican on a campus where most were Democrats. And she held to strong religious beliefs in an atmosphere where many around her were unbelieving. "When you're a scholar and immersed in standards of evidence and methods of proof," she has said, "one learns to navigate with ease the world of academia that says, 'You can believe only what you can see.' I've been totally unflappable in my religious faith, and believe that it is the principal reason for all that I've been able to do. My faith in God is the most important thing. I never shied from telling people that I am a Christian, and I believe that's why I've been optimistic in my life."

Taking on the Impossible

Condoleezza went to work. She was determined to balance the Stanford budget within two years. That was something that most people at Stanford said was impossible. "There was a sort of conventional wisdom," said Condoleezza's longtime friend, Professor Coit Blacker, "that said it couldn't be done, that we just had to live with it."

Doing the impossible—that is, balancing the budget—meant firing teachers and staff people, and cutting back on some services to students. "I always feel bad for the dislocation it causes in people's lives," Condoleezza said later. "When I had to lay people off, I eased the transition for them in any way I could. But sometimes you have to make difficult decisions, and you have to make them stick."

Even as she was firing people, the new provost realized she had to find a way to hire people. For a long time, Stanford's leaders had known they should have more female professors. In several faculty departments, there were no female teachers. At the top levels of administration, Condoleezza herself was the only woman.

Studying the problem, Condoleezza realized that there were so few openings on the faculty because so few professors who had tenure ever decided to leave. In the field of education, tenure is granted to teachers after a trial period that usually lasts several years. It guarantees that professors can keep their jobs as long as they do them well. In reducing staff, the provost had to be careful not to dismiss, except for good reason, anyone who had tenure. To make it possible to hire some top-notch women professors, she created a special fund that paid for new positions on the faculty.

Reviewing Stanford's overall curriculum, Condoleezza found that too few students explored basic courses in the humanities such as the arts, literature, the social sciences, languages, and philosophy. She also discovered that too much emphasis was placed on the history of Western civilization without paying attention to the world's other cultures. "Human history," she said, "has been the story of clashes of civilizations and that is the interesting part about it. I never understood the critique that you should teach only Western civilization."

Condoleezza did not hesitate to criticize the teaching of history in America. "Our students' basic knowledge— names, facts, places, what came first," she said, "is abysmal. Someplace—it's got to be either in high school or college—someone has to teach basic history. I've had too many students not able to get Bismarck in the right century."

She also offered the following advice to history students and teachers: "You need to be able to cross cultural lines. It is great that black history is being brought more into American history, because Africans and Europeans landed here together and built this country together, and the separation of African culture and African history from American culture and American history is just ahistorical. If you're going to read and understand Frederick Douglass, then you'd better understand Thomas Jefferson, because that is who he was referencing."

A 180-degree Change

To address these problems with students' humanities background, Condoleezza started a new core curriculum called Introduction to the Humanities. It offered not only fresh study plans but also such up-to-date elements as interactive projects on the Internet, and final marks based on organized group projects rather than exams. Soon the provost could report to President Casper and the Stanford trustees, "I think the experience that an undergraduate has here in the first two years is just 180 degrees from where it was—much more in touch with faculty members, much more small-group oriented, much more research oriented."

Condoleezza faced student demonstrations during her time as provost. One was a protest over the lack of affordable housing on the campus. The disruption came after the applications of 900 graduate students for on-campus housing were rejected. A thousand students gathered and 100 camped overnight on the campus's central quadrangle. The provost announced plans for new housing, but construction would take two years to complete after Stanford trustees approved it.

Another demonstration was triggered when one of the deans refused tenure to an assistant professor of history. Angry students, believing that affirmative action should sway the dean's decision, demonstrated. Condoleezza upheld the dean, pointing out that "done in the right way, affirmative action can be very helpful," but that it should apply only in searching for and appointing teachers. After that, she noted, the individual should be judged entirely on performance, as she herself had been judged. "Tenure is granted," she said, "to those who have achieved true national distinction in research and excellence in teaching."

On May 10, 1996, Provost Rice had the pleasure of making a major announcement to Stanford's Faculty Senate, whose Planning and Policy Board was responsible for guiding the university's future decisions. The budget deficit, she said, was gone. Not only that, but Stanford was keeping a reserve of $14.5 million. The only problem now, she added, was to control the budget so a deficit did not creep back in.

Political Science, Piano, Pumping Iron

During these busy years as provost, Condoleezza kept her mind and body limber. She insisted on maintaining her teaching techniques in the political science classroom and her keyboard skill at the piano. She played regularly in chamber-music quartets and quintets, even attending summer music workshops with the world-famous Muir String Quartet. "I play almost exclusively chamber music," she said in a radio interview, "and I have to be selective. I don't have that much time to practice. And I do like the social aspects of playing chamber music. I played with orchestras a couple of times and always found it overwhelming."

Not only did the Stanford provost exercise her mind and her pianist fingers, she also made sure she found time at least twice a week to put her 5-foot-8, 140-pound frame

Keeping physically fit has always been a crucial part of Condoleezza's lifestyle. (AFP/Corbis)

through a good physical workout. She became a familiar figure in the college's varsity weight room, pumping iron and running on the treadmill for at least an hour. "I do some of my best thinking on the treadmill," she said.

The world beyond Stanford continued to recognize Condoleezza Rice. She was awarded honorary doctorates by the University of Notre Dame in 1994 and the University of Alabama in 1995. That year J.P. Morgan, one of the nation's oldest investment banking firms, made her a member of its International Advisory Council, where she met international leaders in business and government.

From Preventing Deadly Conflict to Integrating Women Soldiers

Of all such posts, the one that would influence Condoleezza's future most heavily came in 1994. It was her trusteeship on the Carnegie Corporation, one of America's oldest philanthropic organizations. Serving on the advisory council to Carnegie's Commission on Preventing Deadly Conflict, she provided expert insight into the nuclear stockpiles of the former Soviet Union and the United States. Here she shared her views with such world leaders as Mikhail Gorbachev, former U.S. President Jimmy Carter, South African Bishop Desmond Tutu (winner of the 1984 Nobel Peace Prize), and former U.S. Secretary of Defense Robert S. McNamara.

Condoleezza's third book, *Germany Unified and Europe Transformed: A Study in Statecraft,* was published in 1995. She was coauthor with Philip Zelikow, a man who had written several books on the presidency of John F. Kennedy and who had served in President Bush's administration when Germany was being put back together. The book won several awards, including the Akira Iriye International History Book Award, a citation for excellence in nonfiction books on foreign affairs from the Overseas Press Club of America, and a Book of Distinction award from the American Academy of Diplomacy.

The year 1997 brought yet another kind of recognition for Condoleezza. U.S. Secretary of Defense William S. Cohen set up the Federal Advisory Committee on Gender Integrated Training in the Military. Its purpose, he announced, was "to determine how best to train our gender-integrated, all-volunteer force to ensure that they are disciplined, effective, and ready." He asked Provost Rice to serve on the committee.

Once again Condoleezza was involved in creating important government policy on what could be a controversial subject: how to integrate more women into our country's military services. The committee studied and made recommendations in several areas, including instruction on the handling of sexual harassment problems, hiring of additional women trainers, equalizing recruitment opportunities for women and men, improvement of basic training, instruction of drill sergeants, and development of separate barracks for each sex.

Maintaining a Balanced Life

Busy as she was, Condoleezza methodically kept room for religion in her life. In 1997 her pastor at Menlo Park Presbyterian Church invited her to deliver the sermon at all five Sunday services. From the pulpit she told each congregation how, from her earliest childhood, she had received lessons on perseverance and faith. Describing how the wonders of God's world are revealed every day in her spiritual journey, she said, "There is so much more to know. We should wrestle with our faith, questioning and trying to understand better our relationship with God."

Her years as provost of Stanford University gave Condoleezza Rice a reputation as a dynamic teacher and scholar. Yet she was also highly respected as the college's tough-as-nails manager who not only got rid of debt but also produced fresh funding from its patrons. "Condi was not running any popularity contest," Coit Blacker, her longtime teaching associate, later said. "She was effective as provost because of her ability to make tough decisions and stick to them even if they made people unhappy."

6

"BUSH'S SECRET WEAPON"

During her years as provost at Stanford, Condoleezza Rice continued the friendship she had established with George Herbert Walker Bush and his wife, Barbara, when they were president and first lady. In the summer of 1998 the Bushes invited her for a visit at their family home in Kennebunkport, Maine. On this visit Condoleezza first met the Bushes' eldest son, George W. Bush, who was then governor of Texas.

The Bushes had planned a fishing trip for the visit. "I don't get seasick, but I also don't like the water very much," Condoleezza said later, "and I most certainly don't fish. I let President and Governor Bush fish and I sat and talked. We talked a lot about the state of the American armed forces and ballistic missile defense."

Talking with the Texas governor, she noticed he seemed more high-strung than his father. "Governor Bush is some-what more interactive," she said. "He tends to press the speaker to answer questions almost in a kind of rapid-fire manner." Later, commenting on the younger George Bush, she said, "I am immensely fond of him. He is quick in a good way, he has got a very sharp intellect that goes right to the core of something." One further reason for her admiration, she said, was that "we are both sports fans. We got along well right away."

"Try many paths."

The Kennebunkport holiday was a productive one for Condoleezza and the Bushes. It promised many talk-and-think sessions to come. In the meantime the provost continued her leadership at Stanford. In September 1998, just after the Kennebunkport trip, she made a speech to the incoming freshman class. In it she touched on some of her central beliefs about education and life in general.

"Your job here," she told them, "is to find your passion. Not just something that interests you, but something that you cannot live without. I encourage your parents not to panic if you find a passion, such as Etruscan art, that might not get you a job but will glorify your soul. Try many paths. Try something hard. And take time to get to know those around you—particularly those beyond your ethnic, religious, or ideological background."

It was a forward-looking speech. Over the course of the 1998–99 school year Condoleezza thought often about trying another path herself. She was doing her job as provost and keeping up her passions for teaching political science, for playing the piano (she even gave occasional concerts on the campus), and for sports. For example, on the weekend of her birthday that fall, she was a spectator at a Stanford Cardinals football game, a men's basketball game, and a women's basketball tournament—and she also watched the San Francisco 49ers football team on television. But after six intensive years as provost of Stanford University, her active mind was still ranging beyond the college campus.

Three interests were tugging at her. One was the Hoover Institution, with its challenging environment of deep-thinking minds. The second was a different kind of challenge: her work advising the J.P. Morgan banking firm on economic issues that were worldwide in scope. The third was a fast-growing challenge from her friendship with the Bush family: More and more, Condoleezza was aware that Governor Bush of Texas was seriously considering running for president. She wanted to help him.

That spring Condoleezza announced she would resign as provost in June. She would be a senior fellow at Hoover and would be traveling a lot for J.P. Morgan, but she would keep her condominium on campus and her season tickets for Stanford basketball games. She added, "I'm doing some work obviously for Governor Bush."

What some of Condoleezza's associates guessed, if they did not know for certain, was that she was leaving not just to do "some work" for George W. Bush. She was going to

Condoleezza with presidential candidate George W. Bush and campaign foreign policy adviser Paul Wolfowitz, September 2000. (Associated Press)

work for him full time. Stanford's loss, many felt, would be Bush's gain. "We've had a great partnership in the day-to-day work of the university," said Mariann Byerwalter, the college's vice president for business affairs. "She's a quick study and gets to the heart of an issue very quickly."

Condoleezza described her decision this way: "The most important thing became to get back to what I do, which is international politics," she said. "I haven't been to Russia in two and a half years. For me, going to Russia is like breathing."

"Getting asked to do all sorts of things"

Within six months after leaving her Stanford job, Condoleezza Rice was a stalwart member of the team that was planning George W. Bush's nomination campaign. By then readers of *Time* magazine knew that former Secretary of State George Shultz had said of Rice, "She has such a level of capability that she winds up getting asked to do all sorts of things." Basically, of course, she was Bush's chief adviser on foreign policy. It was her job to guide him on America's attitude toward all other countries.

A reporter named Alan Bock interviewed Provost Rice just before she left Stanford in June 1999. "I couldn't help but like her," he said in his report, published the following December. "She is certainly charming . . . and well informed."

They talked about whether NATO (North Atlantic Treaty Organization) was right when it approved the bombing of Yugoslavia that spring. NATO had been trying to stop that country's attempt to drive out ethnic Albanians from its Kosovo region. "As she views matters," Bock reported, "the United States has a natural 'security zone' or sphere-of-influence area that includes Europe and the Middle East. One wouldn't always intervene in every little dispute in that area, she said, and one would want to be sure an intervention would be effective rather than an empty gesture."

Bock noted two things about Condoleezza's comments. First, she was critical of the bombing campaign itself. Second, she did not want the United States and NATO to think that just by dropping bombs from 15,000 feet they could gain their political and diplomatic goals. "Military conflict always entails risks, and usually bigger risks than are at first anticipated," she told Bock. "If we start to get the idea we can have risk-free wars whenever some foreign leader displeases us, we'll be in a lot of trouble."

"The brains of the operation"

In the fall of 1999 Condoleezza was one of 10 people chosen by George W. Bush to serve on his Presidential Exploratory Committee. In an interview on *ABC News,* she said her job was to help the governor with "the very basic work he has wanted to do on the nature of the politics in various countries, the nature of alliances, really laying a lot of the groundwork" for future foreign policy.

By March 2000 it had become clear that in the summer Bush would win the Republican nomination for president. Headlines were calling Condoleezza Rice "Bush's secret weapon." There was talk that, if he were elected, Bush would name her for a top position in his cabinet, the group that includes the heads of the major departments of the U.S. government.

"Rice would be a daring choice for secretary of state," wrote columnist Steve Kettmann of the Internet magazine *Salon*. "If Bush wins, she would be in line for that or another top job. Bush's many foreign-policy gaffes guarantee he will face heavy pressure to prove he's smarter on world affairs than he sounds." The sub-headline above Kettmann's *Salon* article summed up his opinion: "It's clear she's the brains of the operation."

Kettmann noted that Condoleezza saw qualities in Governor Bush that many people did not see. She had said that Bush "came into the discussion of foreign policy with some very strong views already, some very strong values. Free trade is in his bones. He's watched how the North American Free Trade Agreement has improved both the Texan and Mexican economies. I think he has seen how free trade can be a valuable tool."

Over the winter of 2000, as Bush campaigned to win primary elections in state after state, Condoleezza tutored him on foreign policy. She headed the group of writers who created his speech on nuclear strategy. And in the "W is for Women" effort to produce wide support for Bush among women, she was the most prominent female.

Speaking Her Mind

Condoleezza proved she could hold her own during the fights that often arise during political campaigns. In April, before either Bush or then Vice President Al Gore had been formally nominated, the vice president attacked the governor, saying Bush had no expertise in foreign policy. Condoleezza responded by reminding people of how demonstrators had disrupted meetings of the World Trade Organization in Seattle the preceding December. "Where was Gore when it was time to stand up and be counted in Seattle?" she asked. She went on to say that Gore should come out strongly for permanent trade relations with China. "When it comes to the vote on China," she said, "he's been missing in action."

At the Republican National Convention in August 2000 a speech by Condoleezza was a highlight. "Democracy in America is still a work in progress," she told the crowd. "But even with its flaws, this unique American experience provides a shining beacon to peoples who still suffer in places where ethnic difference is a license to kill."

Relating her Granddaddy Rice's experience of getting an education that took him from harvesting cotton to preaching as a Presbyterian minister, she said, "In America, with education and hard work, it really does not matter where you came from, it matters only where you are going. But that truth cannot be sustained if it is not renewed in each generation."

Now came the campaign to defeat the Democratic candidate, Al Gore, for the presidency. Condoleezza not only advised Bush on what positions to take on foreign policy, she expressed her own opinions publicly, as well. For example, she said that criticism from other countries should not keep the United States from developing an antimissile system. She said she hoped Russia would agree to change the 1972 Anti-Ballistic Missile Treaty to permit the American missile defense program to go ahead. If those in Moscow do not agree, she added, the United States should revoke the treaty anyway. Even in the middle of an election campaign, this was strong talk.

In October Condoleezza created a wave of worry among members of NATO. In an interview with the *New York Times*, she said the armies of the European countries should keep the peace in the Balkans. U.S. peacekeepers who were there, she said, should be brought home. The worry at NATO resulted in candidate Bush assuring its secretary-general, Lord Robinson, that America's peacekeepers would stay.

Political writer Jay Nordlinger reported on rumors about Condoleezza's future in the Bush administration. In the magazine *National Review*, he said that if Condoleezza became America's first African-American secretary of state she would be "rock-star big, a major cultural figure, adorning the bedroom walls of innumerable kids and the covers of innumerable magazines."

"I TRUST HER JUDGMENT"

The presidential election in November 2000 was one of the closest in U.S. history. The nationwide popular vote—that is, the number of actual votes cast in voting booths—gave Al Gore the victory by about 540,000 out of the 100 million votes that were cast. But what counts is the vote of the electoral college, a group in which each state has as many electors as it has senators and representatives. Usually each elector votes for the nominee of his or her party. When the popular vote is extremely close, the loser may actually get a majority of electoral votes and thus become the winner. In all of U.S. history, this has happened only three times: in 1876, 1888, and 2000.

In fact, the vote in the electoral college in 2000 depended on the outcome in Florida. There the voting officials declared that Bush had a slight majority of the popular vote, which meant that Republicans would become Florida's members of the electoral college. The

Democrats demanded a recount. The dispute raged for a month until the Supreme Court of the United States stopped the attempted recount. Florida's 25 electoral votes then put George W. Bush in the White House.

"On his list for several positions"

President-elect Bush had already been planning his appointments to cabinet positions and other White House staff jobs. Condoleezza Rice was near the top of his list. "I would think she should be on his list for several positions, certainly national security advisor," said Carla Hills, who had been U.S. trade representative in the earlier Bush administration. She had worked with Condoleezza not only in the White House but also on the Chevron board of directors. "I think her experience as provost at Stanford has given her an interesting window on budgeting and management that is really quite extensive," Hills added. "She is firm, which is maybe a nicer word for tough, and that is because she does her homework and knows her position."

Now a lengthy interview with Condoleezza was made public. Dated back to June 2000, it had been conducted by a visiting scholar from the Transatlantic Information Exchange Service, an organization whose mission is to "strengthen the transatlantic partnership by promoting dialogue among individuals on a people-to-people level."

The discussion revealed how eloquent Condoleezza Rice was on a wide range of subjects. Asked about links between Europeans and Americans she said, "I think that relations are so multifaceted and in so many aspects of life that we have simply ceased to think about it any longer. It has become routine. The tendency of youth to think of themselves as going and working there for three years is probably the best thing we have going for us."

America should not take its allies for granted, Condoleezza added, but should constantly tend to them. "If I never call my friends until I need them," she said, "then the relationship is not going to be very strong when I get there."

"She is a wise person."

On January 15, 2001, Condoleezza resigned from the board of directors of Chevron. On January 18, President-elect George W. Bush announced that Condoleezza Rice would be his national security advisor. "Dr. Rice is not only a brilliant person," said Bush, "she is an experienced person. She is a good manager. I trust her judgment. America will find that she is a wise person."

In England the BBC News quoted Bush as describing Condoleezza as the person "who can explain to me foreign policy matters in a way I can understand." The same broadcast also noted "she has indicated that under the

Bush plan, the U.S. will focus its military energies on the Persian Gulf, Asia, and other regions in which America's national interests are directly involved."

Six days after the president-elect made his announcement, Condoleezza again had to mix personal sorrow with the joy of her new appointment. Her 77-year-old father died of heart failure on Christmas Eve.

On January 22, 2001, two days after President George W. Bush was inaugurated, Condoleezza Rice was officially appointed as the assistant to the president for national security affairs. Her unofficial title was national security advisor. After her appointment Condoleezza made a strong public statement: "George W. Bush will never allow America and our allies to be blackmailed. And make no mistake, blackmail is what the outlaw states seeking long-range ballistic missiles have in mind." Condoleezza stressed that maintaining relations with the United States' allies and creating a missile defense system would be some of the main focuses of Bush's presidency.

Because she had previous experience working in the White House under the new president's father, Condoleezza was hardly a stranger in Washington, D.C. The new vice president, Dick Cheney, had been secretary of defense under the first President Bush. The new secretary of state, Colin Powell, had been chairman of the Joint Chiefs of Staff. Condoleezza had worked closely with both

National Security Advisor Rice talks with Secretary of State Colin Powell. (Associated Press)

of them. But most of the country and world knew little about her. Now, as the national spotlight shone on her, journalists hurried to interview people about the new national security advisor.

One reporter talked with Philip Zelikow, who was director of the Miller Center of Public Affairs at the University of Virginia. He had not only worked with Condoleezza in the White House but also had coauthored a book with her.

"She has a nice combination of three kinds of experience: scholarly intellectual knowledge, real experience working in government, and responsibility for administering a large institution," he said. "This is an unusual combination." He pointed out that previous and famous national security advisors, such as Henry Kissinger, did not have this blend of experience.

"She is pretty levelheaded," concluded Zelikow. "She never displayed an overly large ego, elbowing people out of the way. She never had that kind of reputation at all."

Good reporters get at least two points of view. Some went to the Nixon Center, a Washington think tank concerned with American security. The director of the center, Dimitri K. Simes, is said to know as much about Soviet affairs as Condoleezza. "I am not a close personal friend," said Simes, but he added, "I talk to people at Stanford who do not agree with her politics and are jealous about her rise. They all say she was an impressive provost."

Simes thought of Condoleezza as a rival in expertise. But he said, "I am sure she knows more about some regions than others. But it is more dangerous to think you know something and have it wrong than to realize there are gaps in your information. As long as she realizes that she is stronger in some areas than in others, and I am told she realizes it, that is as good as you can get."

"Stitching the connections together"

Newspapers soon reported that Condoleezza Rice was in full charge at the National Security Council (NSC). She made many changes when she took over, some of them controversial. Within three weeks after the new administration took office, she cut its staff to one third of the more than 100 she had inherited from President Bill Clinton's administration. She shifted the council's emphasis to a strategy that put defense first, including national missile defense. She did something no one else in her position had done when she brought the secretary of the treasury, Paul H. O'Neill, into her regular meetings with Secretary of State Powell and Secretary of Defense Donald H. Rumsfeld.

Next she eliminated several of the NSC's divisions or departments. Gone were specialists on such issues as health and the international environment. People with skills in communications and in dealing with Congress or with state legislatures were dismissed. "What's new is not that the NSC is smaller," said one official. "What's new is what's behind the sizing. It's a view about what the NSC staff ought to be for this president."

Condoleezza made her view clear. She was not there to create policy or set it in motion, she said. Rather, as *Washington Post* staff writers Karen DeYoung and Steven Mufson reported, "She sees her task as making sure Bush is briefed and staffed to play his role in foreign and secu-

Condoleezza meets with Russian president Vladimir Putin in Moscow, 2001. (Associated Press)

rity matters, advancing his strategic agenda while thinking through big issues such as guidelines for foreign intervention, and serving as an honest broker of differences among the major policy players."

The new national security advisor described her job as "working the seams, stitching the connections together tightly, providing glue for the many, many agencies and instruments the United States is now deploying around the world."

She did some high-level stitching herself. During that summer of 2001, she traveled to Moscow. There she was the first senior official of the new administration to meet in private with Vladimir Putin, the president of Russia. She then accepted an invitation to spend the weekend as his guest at his dacha, that is, his summer country cottage.

"IT'S A TERRORIST ATTACK"

The question of America's security became major news around the world on Tuesday morning, September 11, 2001. Here is how Condoleezza later described what she experienced:

> I was standing at my desk in the White House, and I was waiting to go down to my senior staff meeting, when my executive assistant handed me a note that said that a plane had hit the World Trade Center. And my first thought was, what a terrible accident. And I called the president and he said essentially the same thing, he was in Florida, he said, what a terrible accident.
>
> And, of course, first reports are always wrong. First we thought it was a twin-engine plane, and then later

we learned it was a commercial airliner. And I went down for my senior staff meeting and about three people into the staff meeting, as I was asking for reports, I got a note from my executive assistant that said a second plane has hit the World Trade Center. And I thought, my God, it's a terrorist attack.

And I walked into the situation room to try to gather together the national security principals for a session, a meeting, and I was trying to reach Don Rumsfeld and I couldn't. And I looked behind me, and a plane had hit the Pentagon. And there were reports that there were car bombs at the State Department and that airplanes were headed for the White House.

Over the weekend after the attack, President Bush's high-level security officials met at Camp David, the presidential hideaway not far from Washington, D.C. There the group discussed how best to react to the terrorists' actions. Then, following their intensive deliberation, the security experts relaxed with some entertainment. Leading the program was Attorney General John Ashcroft, at the piano, accompanying Condoleezza Rice, as she sang favorite American songs.

Six Truths to Think About

In the shock of the days just after September 11, Condoleezza began to rethink some of the most basic elements of national security. "There are certain verities [truths]," she said later in a major speech at Johns Hopkins University, "that September 11th reinforced and brought home to us in the most vivid way."

The first truth was America's "end to innocence" regarding its vulnerability to terrorist attacks. The attack, she said, "reinforced one of the rediscovered truths about today's world: robust military power matters in international politics and in security."

The second truth, said Condoleezza, was that a sound foreign policy begins at home. That meant improving airport security, tightening requirements for handling the visas of foreign visitors and immigrants, and protecting such infrastructure or basic framework as nuclear power plants and computerized systems.

Third, she pointed out, was the obvious truth that "we can do only so much to protect ourselves at home, and so the best defense is a good offense. We have to take the fight to the terrorists."

Her fourth truth was the need to deny terrorists and hostile states the opportunity to acquire weapons of mass destruction. What that meant, she said, was that "the world's most dangerous people simply cannot be permitted to obtain the world's most dangerous weapons."

Global terror demands a global solution was Condoleezza's fifth truth. "The new challenges," she said, "have underscored the critical importance of allies, partners, and coalitions."

She described number six as "one other important truth from this period: An earthquake of the magnitude of 9/11 can shift the tectonic plates of international politics." The collapse of Soviet power in December 1991, she said, marked the start of such a shift and put the world in a period of change or transition in international politics. The September 11 attack, she thought, probably ended the shift. It opened a new period "not just of grave danger, but of enormous opportunity."

Seeing Age-Old Problems in a New Light

Condoleezza summed up her discussion of the six truths by outlining the work and challenges the United States

President Bush meets with Condoleezza at Camp David after the terrorist attacks of September 11, 2001. (Associated Press)

faced as a result of September 11. She said, "Our goal today is what President Bush has called a balance of power that favors freedom. America today possesses as much power and influence as any nation or entity in the world, and certainly in history. But in stark contrast to the leading powers of centuries past, our ambitions are not territorial."

That is, while the United States and its allies might have to use force to fight terrorism and abuses of power in the months and years after September 11, the ultimate aim would not be to take over other countries. This was different from what other powerful nations had done in the past, when military power and domination often went hand in hand. In the new and transitioning world scene, the United States would have to be careful to place its ultimate goals—democracy, freedom, and basic human rights—at the forefront of any military undertaking.

"People dancing on the streets of Kabul"

Of the 19 members of the al-Qaeda terrorist network who hijacked the four airplanes in the September 11 attack, 15 were from Saudi Arabia. So was their leader, the wealthy Osama bin Laden. Now bin Laden was said to be hiding in Afghanistan, a country where an Islamic group called the Taliban was in control. The Taliban had executed Afghanistan's president and given Islamic religious police the power to enforce extreme codes of behavior and dress that were especially unfair to women.

The United States demanded that the Taliban surrender bin Laden and shut down al-Qaeda. The Taliban said no. With help from Great Britain, the United States then bombed Afghanistan and supported that country's Northern Alliance, which opposed the Taliban. By December 7, the alliance had captured the capital city of Kabul and the Taliban had deserted their last stronghold, the city of Kandahar.

Condoleezza Rice saw these events as proof of the truths she often talked about. "I've watched over the last year and a half how people want to have human dignity worldwide," she said. "We forget that when people are given a choice between freedom and tyranny, they will choose freedom. I remember all the stories before the liberation of Afghanistan that they wouldn't 'get it,' that they were all warlords and it would just be chaos. Then we got pictures of people dancing on the streets of Kabul just because they could listen to music or send their girls to school."

No Beeping in Church

More and more, as the United States recoiled from the shock of the September 11 attack, Condoleezza Rice appeared in public to present the point of view of the Bush administration. Known and admired for her smiling directness and self-assurance, she became a favorite of the Sunday-morning talk shows. Hosts who had anchored news programs for many years found her always able to express herself with both clarity and eloquence.

Sunday mornings, however, were not devoted entirely to appearances on political talk shows. Staff people at the White House had already learned not to page Condoleezza Rice during church services on Sunday, which she still attended faithfully.

"She did herself, the arts and her country proud."

Although the United States and the rest of the world were entering a troubled and unsure time, the fabric of society held strong in other ways. One day in the spring of 2002, Condoleezza had a call from the world-famous cellist Yo-Yo Ma. He was to receive the National Medal of Arts from President Bush, he said, and he had been asked to play for the audience at the presentation in Constitution Hall. He asked Condoleezza to accompany him at the piano.

Following the evening's award presentations, first lady Laura Bush stepped to the microphone. "We close tonight's ceremony," she said, "with a performance by one of our very distinguished honorees, Yo-Yo Ma, who will be accompanied on piano by one of our very distinguished colleagues, Dr. Condoleezza Rice. They will play the adagio movement from Brahms's Sonata for Violin and Piano in D Minor, opus 108, and they'll play it as a prayer for peace."

The performance brought the audience to its feet in an enthusiastic ovation. It also brought approval from such critics as Greg Sandow of the *Wall Street Journal*, who wrote, "It's my pleasure to say that she's very good. Her touch was authoritative, her rhythm firm, her phrasing thoughtful. Afterward, I thought, she looked as if this had been a peak moment in her life, and who could blame her? She seemed thrilled, and had every right to be. She did herself, the arts and her country proud."

9

"A WORLD MORE SOBER AND SADDER"

Over the year following September 11, 2001, Condoleezza worked hard both before the television cameras and behind the scenes at the White House trying to make sense of the events of that horrible day. Reporters and others kept asking how such an attack could have occurred on U.S. soil. Why hadn't our security forces caught on? Why hadn't they warned us? Why hadn't they prevented it? As national security advisor, it was Condoleezza Rice's job to answer these tough questions.

"Something was up."

To reply to such questions, Condoleezza Rice held a major briefing for the press on May 16, 2002. She began by saying that threats "come in many varieties. Very often we have uncorroborated information, sometimes we have corroborated but very general information. It is almost never the case that we have information that is specific as to time, place, or method of attack."

Condoleezza told the reporters that as early as December 2000 the intelligence community had "a clear concern that something was up, that something was coming, but it was principally focused overseas." The concern was in areas of the Middle East, the Arabian Peninsula, and Europe, she said. By June and July of 2001 law enforcement agencies were sending messages to the airlines warning of possible use of explosives in an airport

Condoleezza Rice, President Bush, and Defense Secretary Donald Rumsfeld in September 2001. (Associated Press)

terminal, she added. Condoleezza and her staff held meetings daily, "sometimes twice a day," she said, to make plans for dealing with any number of simultaneous attacks around the world.

She said that before September 11, 2001, the Federal Aviation Administration issued what it called "information circulars" that warned of possible terrorist hijackings. Such hijacking, she noted, was expected to be "traditional," in that "the most important and most likely thing was that terrorists would take over an airliner, holding passengers, and demand the release of one of their operatives."

"There was no specific time, place, or method mentioned," said Condoleezza, adding, "I want to reiterate that during this time, the overwhelming bulk of the evidence was that this was an attack that was likely to take place overseas."

A reporter wanted to know why the American public was not informed about these facts before they got on planes in the summer and fall of the previous year.

"It is always a question of how good the information is and whether putting the information out is a responsible thing to do," said Condoleezza. "This was the most generalized kind of information. There was no time, there was no place, there was no method of attack. You would have risked shutting down the American civil aviation system with such generalized information. I think you would have had to think five, six, seven times about that very, very hard."

"What action was taken?"

In that very important press conference, Condoleezza was facing what many in Washington face: hard-nosed questions from the journalists who report White House news. Some reporters asked why the president had not taken action before an attack had happened. Others asked why Condoleezza and her staff could not make a better prediction about these events. These were some of the hardest questions Condoleezza had to face in her career, but through it all, she stood her ground and defended her actions and those of the government.

One reporter asked a question that was perhaps the toughest and most emotional of the day: "Dr. Rice, there are a lot of widows and widowers and family members of the victims of September 11th who are listening to this, and thinking today that the government let them down, that there were intelligence failures. As the person who is supposed to connect the dots with the NSC for the president, what would you like to say to them today?"

"This government," she responded, "did everything that it could in a period in which the information was very generalized, in which there was nothing specific to which to react. And had this president known of something more specific, or known that a plane was going to be used as a missile, he would have acted on it."

Reporters continued to probe, with more questions about how much the security people knew before September 11. Condoleezza continued to answer with calmness and coolness, and people around the world waited anxiously for her answers. In the end everyone present agreed that in Condoleezza Rice's press briefing they had seen a remarkable example of grace under attack.

Remembering Her Students

Although Condoleezza was busy addressing questions about national security, she did not forget the students back at Stanford. The school's class of 2002 got in touch with her that spring. They asked her if she could spare the time to come to Palo Alto and deliver the commencement day speech on June 16.

Condoleezza could and did. She reminded the new graduates that she had made a speech to them before, during their first week as college freshmen. "Today," she said, "you are stepping into a world that is quite different than the one that existed when you arrived. It is a world that is more sober and sadder—clearer about its vulnerabilities— yet stronger, more conscious of our differences and yet more aware of our humanity."

The former provost urged her listeners to "act on the habits of mind that you have developed here" by accepting three basic responsibilities. First, she said, "Acknowledge that you have an obligation to search for the truth. Ideas matter and they must therefore be subjected to scrutiny and to examination."

The second responsibility, said Condoleezza, is "to be optimistic" about the power of education. She told the crowd how the optimism of her Granddaddy Rice had carried him from the cotton fields to an education. "What my grandfather understood, and what I experienced years later," she said, "is the transforming power of education. And just as education transforms individuals one by one, it can transform whole societies."

Condoleezza also mentioned the powerful example of her role model Fannie Lou Hamer, who had come to the University of Denver to speak to her father's class. "She was not sophisticated in the way we think of it," said Condoleezza, "yet [she was] so compelling that I remember the power of her message even today. In 1964 Fannie Lou Hamer refused to listen to those who told her that a sharecropper with a sixth-grade education could not, or should not, launch a challenge that would dismantle the racist infrastructure of Mississippi's Democratic Party. She did it anyway."

The new graduate's third responsibility is to transform people, Condoleezza continued, which grows out of the

Condoleezza at the Stanford commencement ceremony, 2002.
(L.A. Cicero/Stanford News Service)

power of education. It is the obligation to recognize that cultural differences exist and are "part of what makes the human race vibrant." She said, "What stirs the human soul or bridges the seemingly unbridgeable cultural divide" is "the burning desire for liberty. Given a choice between tyranny and freedom, people will choose freedom."

10

"IT'S TIME FOR THIS TO END"

In the fall of 2002 "security" was an everyday word in Washington, D.C., and around the world. Event after event related to national security, and Condoleezza was either just behind the scenes or visibly active in most of them.

Eliminating Weapons of Mass Destruction

On September 12, in a speech before the United Nations, President Bush said that Iraq and its leader, Saddam Hussein, had repeatedly violated U.N. resolutions that called for the elimination of weapons of mass destruction, an end to the support of terrorism, and the assurance of basic human rights for the Iraqi people. He asked the U.N. to make strict inspections for weapons and to insist on "regime change," or change of government, if Iraq did not cooperate.

The next day, the White House published *The National Security Strategy of the United States of America*, a 35-page document produced by Condoleezza Rice's office. This document presented a plan by which the United States, in order to protect basic human freedoms at home and abroad, would "act against . . . emerging threats," which included terrorism and weapons of mass destruction, with military force, if necessary.

In issuing the strategy, some said the United States was taking a bold new step: It was telling the rest of the world how to behave. The writer and editor of the message was Condoleezza Rice.

In an interview later that year, Condoleezza defended this controversial document by saying, "I think if you go through history, you can make a very strong argument that it was not acting, or acting too late, that has had the greatest consequences for international politics—not the other way around. We all live with the specter of World War II, and we all live with the fact that the great democracies were not able to muster the will to act even when the handwriting was pretty clear on the wall that Adolf Hitler was unstoppable except by force."

The message was indeed becoming very clear: The United States wanted to put an end to terrorist networks and the creation of weapons of mass destruction in Iraq, and it would be willing to wage a war to do so.

Accompanying British Prime Minister Tony Blair to President Bush's ranch in Crawford, Texas, 2002. (Associated Press)

Moving Toward War

Now the U.N. was considering how to respond to President Bush's request for weapons inspections in Iraq. While the U.N. Security Council was debating, the U.S. Congress passed a resolution on October 11 that authorized President Bush to use force in Iraq. This meant that the president could start a war despite the U.S. Constitution's rule that Congress holds the power "to declare war."

On November 8, the U.N. Security Council unanimously passed Resolution 1441, which called for U.N. weapons inspectors in Iraq. The resolution also reminded Iraq of the council's repeated warnings that more Iraqi violations of U.N. resolutions would bring serious consequences.

Over the next three months, U.N. inspectors made several trips to Iraq in search of weapons of mass destruction. However, they could not find any. In the United States, tensions mounted and a military action against Iraq began to look more likely.

A Controversial Decision

One thing that Condoleezza had learned long ago in Washington was that no matter how busy people were with one subject, such as the weapons inspections in Iraq, there was always something else happening. On Wednesday, January 16, 2003, President Bush announced that he would support two lawsuits brought before the U.S. Supreme Court to end an affirmative action program at the University of Michigan. Affirmative action was a policy of the university that tried to make sure the student body was diverse by giving extra consideration to applicants whose backgrounds were African-American, Latino, or Native American.

The next day, two briefs filed with the Supreme Court by the Bush administration claimed the Michigan policy was "plainly unconstitutional" and was the same thing as a racial quota. The White House briefs said Michigan officials "cannot justify the express consideration of race in their admissions policy."

Reporters hurried to find out who had advised the president on taking his stand. They learned from Bush aides that Condoleezza Rice had been one of a handful of advisers who met more than two dozen times over the preceding month to discuss the case. One reporter wrote: "The officials said Rice, in a series of lengthy one-on-one meetings with Bush, drew on her experience as provost at Stanford University to help convince him that favoring minorities was not an effective way of improving diversity on college campuses."

Black leaders criticized the president's decision. Condoleezza, according to reporters, was angered by the newspaper stories because she thought they were written because she is black. On January 17, with Bush's permission, she issued a statement. It said, "I agree with the president's position, which emphasizes the need for diversity and recognizes the continued legacy of racial prejudice, and the need to fight it. The president challenged universities to develop ways to diversify their populations fully. I believe that while race-neutral means are preferable, it is appropriate to use race as one factor among others in achieving a diverse student body."

Even though she faced criticism from minority groups because of her controversial position on this issue, Condoleezza once again proved her ability to defend herself eloquently and forcefully.

The Iraq War

By March 2003, in the United States and around the world, tension over the situation in Iraq was building. After months of weapons inspections with no results, President Bush was coming closer to ordering military action against Iraq. Several members of the U.N. Security Council wanted to pass another resolution that would allow more time for weapons inspections. In regard to these requests Condoleezza Rice echoed the words of President Bush and many others when she said, "It's time for this to end."

On March 17, in a major address to the nation, President Bush gave Saddam Hussein and his sons 48 hours to leave Iraq before military action began. Hussein rejected the ultimatum.

On March 19, 2003, the United States and allied forces from Great Britain, Poland, Australia, and other nations declared war on Iraq.

Protest and Conviction

During these events in March, demonstrators in cities across America, as well as in other countries, expressed their dismay that for the first time in its history the United States was starting a war.

Condoleezza Rice stood by the president's decision to take action against Iraq. In an interview on an Australian news website, she spoke about Secretary of State Colin Powell's presentation to the United Nations, in which he offered evidence of Iraq's possession of weapons of mass destruction. "I hope that the people of Australia had a chance to watch Secretary Powell's very careful presentation of the facts of this case," she said, "because you could not come away from that presentation with any other conclusion but that Saddam Hussein has no intention to disarm, that he is a very dangerous man holding on to stocks of weapons of mass destruction. . . ."

"The coalition would have
the leading role."

By early April it was clear the war would end quickly. Debate began over whether the United States or the United Nations should take the leading role in the creation of a new government for Iraq. On April 4 the foreign ministers of Russia, Germany, and France—the leading countries that had refused to support the coalition—met in Paris. They issued a joint statement calling for the United Nations to play the "central role" in creating a new Iraq.

Condoleezza summoned reporters to a White House press conference that afternoon. With typical directness, she let the countries that had not fought Hussein know that they could not expect to determine what sort of government followed him. "It would only be natural," she said, "to expect that after having participated and having liberated Iraq, coalition forces, having given life and blood to liberate Iraq, that the coalition would have the leading role."

She then made it clear that President Bush intended to see two kinds of Iraqis in the new government: those who had been out of that country as exiles, and those who had just been freed because of the war. Once again, National Security Advisor Condoleezza Rice was speaking with authority.

Condoleezza shakes hands with United Nations Secretary General Kofi Annan, 2003. (Associated Press)

What's Next?

What does the future hold for Condoleezza Rice? Making predictions is never easy, but at least two future possibilities for the national security advisor have been suggested.

The first is football. Everybody knows what a big football fan Condoleezza is. She is one of the game's greatest fanatics. More than once she has suggested that her dream job would be commissioner of the National Football League.

But there is a job even bigger than that: president of the United States. Condoleezza has denied that she's interested in running for the presidency, but many people think differently. Time will tell if she will one day launch a campaign of her own.

Regardless of her political future, one thing is certain about Condoleezza Rice: She continues to be prominent in national affairs and events. With her intelligence, determination, and signature grace under pressure, Condoleezza has made a powerful impact in whatever she has done, from playing the piano, to administering a large university, to serving as a top presidential advisor during a time of war. Whatever path she chooses to take in the future, one can be sure that she will get there through a belief she has held her entire life: one person's ability can make a world of difference.

TIME LINE

1954 Condoleezza Rice is born November 14, in Birmingham, Alabama.

1958 Plays her first piano recital

1963 Watches civil rights marchers; hears the bomb blast that kills four girls, including a friend, at Sunday school

1965 Reaches the eighth grade at age 11; moves to Denver, Colorado

1968 Hears Fannie Lou Hamer tell about getting black delegates included in the 1964 Democratic National Convention

1970 Enters college at age 15

1971 In Professor Josef Korbel's class, discovers political science; decides not to major in music

1974   Graduates from the University of Denver cum laude
and with Phi Beta Kappa key

1975   Earns master of arts degree in government at the
University of Notre Dame

1980   Switches her party affiliation from Democrat to
Republican

1981   Earns her Ph.D. in international studies at the
University of Denver; wins a fellowship in Stanford
University's Center for International Security and
Arms Control; is appointed an assistant professor of
political science

1984   Wins the Walter J. Gore Award for Excellence in
Teaching; publishes her first book, *The Soviet Union
and the Czechoslovak Army, 1948-1983: Uncertain
Allegiance*

1985   Is appointed a national fellow at the Hoover
Institution

1986   Coauthors the book *The Gorbachev Era* with
Alexander Dallin; wins an International Affairs
Fellowship offered by the Council on Foreign
Relations, serving in the Pentagon as special assis-
tant to the director at the Joint Chiefs of Staff office

1987   Returns to Stanford

1989   Is appointed as the National Security Council's
director of Soviet and Eastern Affairs, then senior
director and special assistant to President George
Herbert Walker Bush; tours Poland and Hungary
and attends the "Malta Summit" with Bush; meets
Soviet Union president Mikhail Gorbachev

1991   Returns to Stanford; is elected to the boards of
directors at Chevron, Transamerica, Hewlett-
Packard

1993   Christens a Chevron tanker named for her; is
named a full professor at Stanford at age 38; is
named the provost of Stanford

1994   Named a trustee of the Carnegie Corporation

1995   Publishes her third book, *Germany Unified and
Europe Transformed: A Study in Statecraft,* with
Philip Zelikow

1997   Serves on the Federal Advisory Committee on
Gender Integrated Training in the Military

1998   At the Bush home at Kennebunkport, Maine, has
her first political discussions with Texas Governor
George W. Bush

1999   Resigns as provost to become the foreign-policy adviser to presidential candidate Bush

2000   Speaks before the Republican National Convention; after election, is named as President-elect Bush's national security advisor

2001   Reorganizes the National Security Council; in Russia, meets with President Putin; on September 11, is the first to tell President Bush about the attack on the World Trade Center; appears frequently on Sunday talk shows and other news interviews

2002   At the piano, accompanies cellist Yo-Yo Ma at the National Medal of Arts award ceremony; holds a major press briefing on the subject of security lapses before September 11; publishes *The National Security Strategy of the United States of America.*

2003   Advises President Bush on filing an amicus curiae brief with the U.S. Supreme Court concerning the University of Michigan's affirmative action program on college admissions; during the war with Iraq, makes diplomatic visit to Russian president Putin in Moscow

HOW TO BECOME A COLLEGE ADMINISTRATOR

THE JOB

A college administrator's work is demanding and diverse. An administrator is responsible for a wide range of tasks in areas such as counseling services, admissions, alumni affairs, financial aid, academics, and business. The following are some of the different types of college administrators, but keep in mind that this is only a partial list. It takes many administrators in many different departments to run a college.

Many college and university administrators are known as *deans*. Deans are the administrative heads of specific divisions or groups within the university, and are in charge of overseeing the activities and policies of that division. One type of dean is an *academic dean.* Academic deans are concerned with such issues as the requirements for a major, the courses offered, and the faculty hired within a specific academic department or division. The field of academic dean includes such titles as dean of the college of humanities, dean of social and behavioral sciences, and dean of the graduate school, just to name a few. The *dean of students* is responsible for the student-affairs program, often including such areas as student housing, organizations, clubs, and activities.

Registrars prepare class schedules and final exam schedules. They maintain computer records of student data, such as grades and degree requirements. They prepare school catalogs and student handbooks. *Associate registrars* assist in running the school registrar's office.

Recruiters visit high school campuses and college fairs to provide information about their school and to interest students in applying for admission. They develop relationships with high school administrators and arrange to meet with counselors, students, and parents.

Financial aid administrators direct the scholarship, grant, and loan programs that provide financial assistance to students and help them meet the costs of tuition, fees, books, and other living expenses. The administrator keeps students informed of the financial assistance available to them and helps answer student and parent questions and concerns. At smaller colleges, this work might be done by a single person, the *financial aid officer.* At larger colleges and universities, the staff might be bigger, and the financial aid officer will head a department and direct the activities of *financial aid counselors,* who handle most of the personal contact with students.

Other college administrators include *college admissions counselors,* who review records, interview prospective students, and process applications for admission. *Alumni directors* oversee the alumni associations of colleges and universities. An alumni director maintains relationships with the graduates of the college primarily for fund-raising purposes.

Such jobs as university *president, vice president,* and *provost* are among the highest-ranking college and university administrative positions. Generally the president and vice president act as high-level managers, overseeing the rest of a college's administration. They handle business concerns, press relations, public image, and community involvement, and they listen to faculty and administration concerns, often casting the final vote on issues such as compensation, advancement, and tenure. At most schools, the provost is in charge of the many collegiate deans. Working through the authority of the deans, the provost manages the college faculty. The provost also oversees budgets, the academic schedule, event planning, and participates in faculty hiring and promotion decisions.

REQUIREMENTS

High School

A good, well-rounded education is important for anyone pursuing some of the top administrative positions. To prepare for a job in college administration, take accounting and math courses, as you may be dealing with financial records and student statistics. To be a dean of a college, you must have good communication skills, so you should take courses in English literature and composition. Also, speech courses are important, as you will be required to give presentations and represent your department at meetings and conferences. Follow your guidance counselor's college preparatory plan, which will likely include courses in science, foreign language, history, and sociology.

Postsecondary Training

Education requirements for jobs in college administration depend on the size of the school and the job position. Some assistant positions may not require anything more than a few years of experience in an office. For most jobs in college administration, however, you will need at least a bachelor's degree. For the top administrative positions, you will need a master's or a doctorate. A bachelor's degree in any field is usually acceptable for pursuing this career. After you have received your bachelor's, you may choose to pursue a master's in student personnel, administration, or subjects such as economics, psychology, and sociology. Other important studies include education, counseling, information processing, business, and finance. In order to become a college dean, you will need a doctoral degree and many years of experience with a college or university. Your degree may be in your area of study or in college administration.

Other Requirements

As a college administrator, you should be very organized and able to manage a busy office of assistants. Some offices require more organization than others; for example, a financial aid office handles the records and aid disbursement for the entire student body and requires a director with an eye for efficiency and the ability to keep track of all the various sources of student funding. As a dean, however, you will work in a smaller office, concentrating more on issues concerning faculty and committees, and you will rely on your diplomatic skills for maintaining an efficient and successful department. People skills are valuable for college deans, as you will be representing your department both within the university and at national conferences.

Whatever the administrative position, it is important to have patience and tact to handle a wide range of personalities as well as an emotional steadiness when confronted with unusual and unexpected situations.

EXPLORING

To learn something about what the job of administrator entails, talk to your high school principal and superintendent. Also, interview administrators at colleges and universities. Many of their office phone numbers are listed in college directories. The E-mail addresses of the administrators of many different departments, from deans to registrars, are often published on college websites. You should also discuss the career with the college recruiters who visit your high school. Familiarize yourself with all the various aspects of running a college and university by looking at college student handbooks and course catalogs. Most handbooks list all the offices and administrators and how they assist students and faculty.

EMPLOYERS

Administrators are needed all across the country to run colleges and universities. Job opportunities exist at public and private institutions, community colleges, and universities both large and small. In a smaller college, an administrator may run more than one department. There are more job openings for administrators in universities serving large student bodies.

STARTING OUT

There are several different types of entry-level positions available in the typical college administrative office. If you can gain part-time work or an internship in admissions or another office while you are still in school, you will have a great advantage when seeking work in this field after graduation. Any other experience in an administrative or managerial position, which involves working with people or with computerized data, is also helpful. Entry-level positions often involve filing, data processing, and updating records or charts. You might also move into a position as an administrator after working as a college professor. Deans in colleges and universities have usually worked many years as tenured professors.

The department of human resources in most colleges and universities maintains a listing of job openings at the institution and will often advertise the positions nationally. The *Chronicle of Higher Education* (www.chronicle.com) is a newspaper with national job listings. The College and University Professional Association for Human Resources (CUPA-HR) also maintains a job list.

ADVANCEMENT

Entry-level positions, which usually require only a bachelor's degree, include *admissions counselors,* who advise students regarding admissions requirements and decisions, and *evaluators,* who check high school transcripts and college transfer records to determine whether applying students may be admitted. Administrative assistants are hired for the offices of registrars, financial aid departments, and deans.

Advancement from any of these positions will depend on the manner in which an office is organized as well as how large it is. One may move up to assistant director or associate director, or, in a larger office, into any specialized divisions such as minority admissions, financial aid counseling, or disabled student services. Advancement also may come through transferring to other departments, schools, or systems.

Workshops and seminars are available through professional associations for those interested in staying informed and becoming more knowledgeable in the field, but it is highly unlikely that an office employee will gain the top administrative level without a graduate degree.

EARNINGS

Salaries for college administrators vary widely among two-year and four-year colleges and among public and private institutions, but they are generally comparable to those of college faculty. According to the U.S. Department of Labor's *2001 National Occupational Employment and Wage Estimates,* the median salary for education administrators was $61,700. The lowest-paid 10 percent of administrators earned $33,640 per year, while the highest-paid made $112,620 annually.

According to findings by the CUPA-HR, the following academic deans had these median annual salaries for 2000–01: dean of medicine, $272,200; dean of engineering, $146,938; dean of arts and sciences, $94,666; and dean of mathematics, $69,449. The CUPA-HR also reports the median annual salary for registrars as $58,241, for dean of students as $67,000, and for director of student activities as $39,292.

According to a study done by the *Chronicle of Higher Education,* the average pay for college presidents was $207,000 a year in 2000. Though college presidents can earn high salaries, they are often not as high as earnings of other top administrators and even some college coaches. For example, competition can drive up the pay for highly desired medical specialists, economics educators, or football coaches.

Most colleges and universities provide excellent benefits packages including health insurance, paid vacation, sick leave, and tuition remission. Higher-level administrators such as presidents, deans, and provosts often receive such bonuses as access to special university clubs, tickets to sporting events, expense accounts for entertaining university guests, and other privileges.

WORK ENVIRONMENT

College and universities are usually pleasant places to be employed. Offices are often spacious and comfortable, and the campus may be a scenic, relaxing work setting.

Employment in most administrative positions is usually on a 12-month basis. Many of the positions, such as admissions director, financial aid counselor, and dean of students, require a great deal of direct contact with students, and so working hours may vary according to student needs. It is not unusual for college administrators to work long hours during peak enrollment periods, such as the beginning of each quarter or semester. During these periods, the office can be fast-paced and stressful as administrators work to assist as many students as possible. Directors are sometimes required to work evenings and weekends to provide broader student access to administrative services. In addition, administrators are sometimes required to travel to other colleges, career fairs, high schools, and professional conferences to provide information about the school for which they work.

OUTLOOK

The U.S. Department of Labor predicts that overall employment for education administrators will grow about as fast as the average through 2010. Competition for these prestigious positions, however, will be stiff. Many faculty at institutions of higher learning have the educational and experience requirements for these jobs. Candidates may face less competition for positions in nonacademic areas, such as admissions or fund-raising. Those who are already working within a department seeking an administrator and those willing to relocate will have the best chances of getting administrative positions.

TO LEARN MORE ABOUT COLLEGE ADMINISTRATORS

BOOKS

Bowen, William G., and Harold T. Shapiro, eds. *Universities and Their Leadership.* Princeton, N.J.: Princeton University Press, 1998.

Goldsmith, John A., John Komlos, and Penny Schine Gold. *The Chicago Guide to Your Academic Career: A Portable Mentor for Scholars from Graduate School Through Tenure.* Chicago: University of Chicago Press, 2001.

Jossey-Bass Editors. *The Jossey-Bass Reader on Educational Leadership.* San Francisco: Jossey-Bass, 2000.

WEBSITES

American Association of University Administrators
www.aaua.org

AAUA helps develop standards for college and university administrators through a series of conferences and publications each year. Check the website for more details.

College and University Professional Association for Human Resources

www.cupahr.org

CUPA-HR serves more than 1,600 colleges and universities in the development of human resources programs and processes. They help ensure that the right people find the right jobs in university administration.

Inter-American Organization for Higher Education

www.oui-iohe.qc.ca

This organization is committed to developing partnerships among colleges and universities around the globe for the promotion of higher education. College administrators are heavily involved in this effort.

WHERE TO WRITE

American Association of University Administrators

PO Box 261363

Plano, TX 75026-1363

College and University Professional Association for Human Resources
1233 20th Street, NW, Suite 301
Washington, DC 20036-1250
202-429-0311

INTER-AMERICAN ORGANIZATION FOR HIGHER EDUCATION

Inter-American Organization for Higher Education
Édifice Vieux Séminaire, local 1244
1, Côte de La Fabrique
Québec, Qc, CANADA
G1R 3V6

HOW TO BECOME A FEDERAL OR STATE OFFICIAL

THE JOB

When electing a government official, voters take many different things into consideration. Whether you are electing a new governor and lieutenant governor for the state, a president and vice president for the country, or senators and representatives for the state legislature or the U.S. Congress, voters are choosing people to act on behalf of their interests. The decisions of state and federal lawmakers affect your daily life and your future. State and federal officials pass laws concerning the arts, education, taxes, employment, health care, and other areas, in efforts to change and improve communities and standards of living.

Besides the *president* and *vice president* of the United States, the executive branch of the national government consists of the president's cabinet, including, among others, the secretaries of state, treasury, defense, interior, agriculture, homeland security, and health and human services. These officials are appointed by the president and approved by the Senate. The members of the Office of Management and Budget, the Council of Economic Advisors, and the National Security Council are also executive officers of the national government.

Nearly every state's governing body resembles that of the federal government. Just as the U.S. Congress is composed of the Senate and the House of Representatives, each state (with one exception, Nebraska) has a senate and a house. The executive branch of the U.S. government is headed by the president and vice president, while the states elect governors and lieutenant governors. The *governor* is the chief executive officer of a state. In all states, a large government administration handles a variety of functions related to agriculture, highway and motor vehicle supervision, public safety and corrections, regulation of intrastate business and industry, and some aspects of education, public health, and welfare. The governor's job is to manage this administration. Some states also have a *lieutenant governor,* who serves as the presiding officer of the state's senate. Other elected officials commonly include a secretary of state, state treasurer, state auditor, attorney general, and superintendent of public instruction.

State senators and *state representatives* are the legislators elected to represent the districts and regions of cities and counties within the state. The number of members of a state's legislature varies from state to state. In the U.S. Congress, there are 100 senators (as established by the Constitution—two senators from each state) and 435 representatives. The number of representatives each state is allowed to send to the U.S. Congress varies based on the state's population as determined by the national census. Based on results from Census 2000, California is the most populous state and sends the most representatives (53). The primary function of all legislators, on both the state and national levels, is to make laws. With a staff of aides, senators and representatives attempt to learn as much as they can about the bills being considered. They research legislation, prepare reports, meet with constituents and interest groups, speak to the press, and discuss and debate legislation on the floor of the House or Senate. Legislators also may be involved in selecting other members of the government, supervising the government administration, appropriating funds, impeaching executive and judicial officials, and determining election procedures, among other activities. A state legislator may be involved in examining such situations as the state's relationship to Native American tribes, the level of school violence, and welfare reform.

"Time in each day goes by so quickly," says Don Preister, who serves on the state legislature in Nebraska, "there's no time to read up on all legislation and all the information the constituents send in." The state of Nebraska is the only state with a single-house system. When the state senate is in session, Preister commits many hours to discussing and debating issues with other state senators and gathering information on proposed legislation. In addition to senate sessions, Preister attends committee hearings. His committees include Natural Resources and Urban Affairs. "A hearing lasts from 20 minutes to three or four hours," he says, "depending on the intensity of the issues." Despite having to devote about 60 hours a week to the job when the Senate is in session, Preister finds his work a wonderful opportunity to be of service to the community and to improve lives. "I take a lot of personal satisfaction from being a voice for people whose voices aren't often heard in government."

REQUIREMENTS
High School
Courses in government, civics, and history will give you an understanding of the structure of state and federal gov-

ernments. English courses are important because you need good writing skills for communicating with constituents and other government officials. Math and accounting help you to develop the analytical skills needed for examining statistics and demographics. You should take science courses because you will be making decisions concerning health, medicine, and technological advances. Journalism classes will help you learn about the print and broadcast media and the role they play in politics.

Postsecondary Training

State and federal legislators come from all walks of life. Some hold master's degrees and doctorates, while others have only a high school education. Although a majority of government officials hold law degrees, others have undergraduate or graduate degrees in such areas as journalism, economics, political science, history, and English. Regardless of your major as an undergraduate, it is important to take classes in English literature, statistics, foreign language, Western civilization, and economics. Graduate studies can focus more on one area of study; some prospective government officials pursue master's degrees in public administration or international affairs. Consider participating in an internship program that will involve you with local and state officials. Contact the offices of your state legislators and of your state's members of Congress to apply for internships directly.

Other Requirements

"You should have concern for people," Don Preister says. "You should have an ability to listen and understand people and their concerns." This attention to the needs of communities should be of foremost importance to anyone pursuing a government office. Although historically some politicians have had questionable purposes in their campaigns for office, most successful politicians are devoted to making positive changes and improvements. Good people skills will help you make connections, get elected, and make things happen once in office. You should also enjoy argument, debate, and opposition—you will get a lot of it as you attempt to get laws passed. A good temperament in such situations will earn you the respect of your colleagues. Strong character and a good background will help you to avoid the personal attacks that occasionally accompany government office.

EXPLORING

If you are 16 or older, you can gain experience in a legislature. The U.S. Congress and possibly your state legislature offer opportunities for young adults who have demonstrated a commitment to government study to work as *pages*. For Congress, pages run messages across Capitol Hill, and have the opportunity to see senators and representatives debating and discussing bills. The length of a page's service can be for one summer or up to one year. Contact your state's senator or representative for an application.

You can also explore government careers by becoming involved with local elections. Many candidates for local and state offices welcome young people to assist with campaigns. You might be asked to make calls, post signs, or hand out information about the candidate. Not only will you get to see the politician at work, but you will also meet others with an interest in government.

Another great way to learn about government is to become involved in an issue of interest to you. Participate with a grassroots advocacy group or read about the bills up for vote in the state legislature and U.S. Congress. When you feel strongly about an issue and are well educated on the subject, contact the offices of state legislators and members of Congress to express your views. Visit the websites of the House and Senate and of your state legislature to read about bills, schedules, and the legislators. The National Conference of State Legislators (NCSL) also hosts a website (www.ncsl.org) featuring legislative news and links to state legislatures.

EMPLOYERS

State legislators work for the state government, and many hold other jobs as well. Because of the part-time nature of some legislative offices, state legislators may hold part-time jobs or own their own businesses. Federal officials work full-time for the Senate, the House, or the executive branch.

STARTING OUT

There is no direct career path for state and federal officials. Some enter into their positions after some success with political activism on the grassroots level. Others work their way up from local government positions to state legislature and into federal office. Those who serve as U.S. Congress members have worked in the military, journalism, academics, business, and many other fields.

Many politicians get their start assisting someone else's campaign or advocating for an issue. Don Preister's beginnings with the Nebraska state legislature are particularly inspiring. Because of his involvement in grassroots organizing to improve his neighborhood, he was encouraged by friends and neighbors to run for senator of the district. Others, however, believed he would never get elected running against a man who had had a lot of political success, as well as great finances to back his campaign. "I didn't have any money," Preister says, "or any experience in campaigning. So I went door-to-door to meet the people of the district. I went to every house and apartment in the district." He won that election in 1992 and won again in 1996 and 2000.

ADVANCEMENT

Initiative is one key to success in politics. Advancement can be rapid for someone who is a fast learner and is independently motivated, but a career in politics most often takes a long time to establish. Most state and federal officials start by pursuing training and work experience in their particular field, while getting involved in politics at the local level. Many people progress from local politics to state politics. It is not uncommon for a state legislator to eventually run for a seat in Congress. Appointees to the president's cabinet and presidential and vice presidential candidates frequently have held positions in Congress.

EARNINGS

In general, salaries for government officials tend to be lower than what the official could make working in the private sector. In the case of state legislators, the pay can be very much lower.

The Bureau of Labor Statistics reports that the median annual earning of government legislators was $14,650 in 2001. Salaries generally ranged from less than $11,830 to more than $64,890, although some officials earn nothing at all.

According to the NCSL, state legislators make from $10,000 to $47,000 a year. A few states, however, do not pay state legislators anything but an expense allowance. But a state's executive officials get paid better: *The Book of the States* lists salaries of state governors as ranging from $60,000 in Arkansas to a high of $130,000 in New York.

In 2001 U.S. senators and representatives earned $145,100; the Senate and House majority and minority leaders earned $161,200; the vice president was paid $186,300; and the president earned $400,000.

Congressional leaders such as the Speaker of the House and the Senate majority leader receive higher salaries than the other Congress members. The Speaker of the House makes $186,300 a year. United States Congress members receive excellent insurance, vacation, and other benefits.

WORK ENVIRONMENT

Most government officials work in a typical office setting. Some may work a regular 40-hour week, while others will typically work long hours and weekends. One potential drawback to political life, particularly for the candidate running for office, is that there is no real off-duty time. One is continually under observation by the press and public, and the personal lives of candidates and officeholders are discussed frequently in the media.

Because these officials must be appointed or elected in order to keep their jobs, the ability to determine long-range job objectives is slim. There may be extended periods of unemployment, when living off of savings or working at other jobs may be necessary.

Frequent travel is involved in campaigning and in holding office, so some people with children may find the lifestyle demanding on their families.

OUTLOOK

The U.S. Department of Labor predicts that employment of federal and state officials will grow about as fast as the average through 2010. To attract more candidates to run for legislative offices, states may consider salary increases and better benefits for state senators and representatives. But changes in pay and benefits for federal officials are unlikely. An increase in the number of representatives is possible as the U.S. population grows, but would require additional office space and other costly expansions. For the most part, the structures of state and federal legislatures will remain unchanged, although the topic of limiting the number of terms that a representative is allowed to serve does often arise in election years.

The federal government has made efforts to shift costs to the states; if this continues, it could change the way state legislatures and executive officers operate with regard to public funding. Already, welfare reform has resulted in state governments looking for financial aid in handling welfare cases and job programs. Arts funding may also become the sole responsibility of the states as the National Endowment for the Arts loses support from Congress.

With the government's commitment to developing a place on the Internet, contacting your state and federal representatives, learning about legislation, and organizing grassroots advocacy have become much easier. This voter awareness of candidates, public policy issues, and legislation will increase and may affect how future representatives make decisions. Also look for government programming to be part of cable television's expansion into digital broadcasting. New modes of communication will allow constituents to become even more involved in the actions of their representatives.

TO LEARN MORE ABOUT FEDERAL AND STATE OFFICIALS

BOOKS

Axelrod-Contrada, Joan, and John Kerry. *Career Opportunities in Politics, Government, and Activism.* New York: Facts On File, 2003.

Camenson, Blythe. *Real People Working in Government. (On the Job Series.)* New York: McGraw-Hill, 1998.

Georgetown University School of Foreign Service. *Careers in International Affairs.* 7th ed. Washington, D.C.: Georgetown University Press, 2003.

Ginsberg, Benjamin, et al. *We the People: An Introduction to American Politics.* New York: Norton, 2003.

Woll, Peter, ed. *American Government: Readings and Cases.* 13th ed. Boston: Addison-Wesley, 1998.

WEBSITES

U.S. Senate

www.senate.gov

U.S. House of Representatives

www.house.gov

Visit the Senate and House websites for extensive information about Congress, government history, current legislation, and links to state legislature sites.

National Conference of State Legislatures (NCSL)

www.ncsl.org

To read about state legislatures, policy issues, legislative news, and other related information, visit the NCSL's website.

WHERE TO WRITE

U.S. Senate

Office of Senator (Name)

United States Senate

Washington, DC 20510

202-224-3121

U.S. House of Representatives

Office of the Honorable (Name)

Washington, DC 20515

202-224-3121

National Conference of State Legislatures (NCSL)

444 North Capitol Street, NW, Suite 515

Washington, DC 20001

202-624-5400

HOW TO BECOME
A MUSICIAN

THE JOB

Instrumental musicians play one or more musical instruments, usually in a group and in some cases as featured soloists. Musical instruments are usually classified in several distinct categories according to the method by which they produce sound: strings (violins, cellos, and basses, for example), which make sounds by vibrations from bowing or plucking; woodwinds (oboes, clarinets, saxophones), which make sounds by air vibrations through reeds; brass (trumpets, French horns, trombones, and so on), which make sounds by air vibrations through metal; and percussion (drums, pianos, triangles), which produce sound when they are struck. Instruments can also be classified as electric or acoustic, especially in popular music. Synthesizers are another common instrument, and computer and other electronic technology increasingly is used for creating music.

Musicians may play in symphony orchestras, dance bands, jazz bands, rock bands, country bands, or other groups, or they might go it alone. Some musicians may play in recording studios either with their group or as a session player for a particular recording. Recordings are in the form of records, tapes, compact discs, DVDs, and videotape cassettes. *Classical musicians* perform in concerts, opera performances, and chamber music concerts, and they may also play in theater orchestras, although theater music is not normally classical. The most talented performers may work as soloists with orchestras or alone in recitals. Some classical musicians accompany singers and choirs, and they may also perform in churches and temples.

Instrumental musicians and singers use their skills to convey the form and meaning of written music. They work to achieve precision, fluency, and emotion within a piece of music, whether through an instrument or through their own voice. Musicians practice constantly to perfect their techniques.

Many musicians supplement their incomes through teaching while others teach as their full-time occupation, perhaps playing jobs occasionally. *Voice and instrumental music teachers* work in colleges, high schools, elementary schools, conservatories, and in their own studios; often they give concerts and recitals featuring their students. Many professional musicians give private lessons.

Students learn to read music, develop their voices, breathe correctly, and hold their instruments properly.

Individuals also write and prepare music for themselves or other musicians to play and sing. _Composers_ write the original music for symphonies, songs, or operas using musical notation to express their ideas through melody, rhythm, and harmony. _Arrangers_ and _orchestrators_ take a composer's work and transcribe it for the various orchestra sections or individual instrumentalists and singers to perform; they prepare music for film scores, musical theater, television, or recordings. _Copyists_ assist composers and arrangers by copying down the various parts of a composition, each of which is played by a different section of the orchestra. _Librettists_ write words to opera and musical theater scores, and _lyricists_ write words to songs and other short musical pieces. A number of _songwriters_ compose both music and lyrics, and many are musicians who perform their own songs.

REQUIREMENTS
High School

If you are interested in becoming a musician, you will probably need to develop your musical skills long before you enter high school. While you are in high school, however, there are a number of classes you can take that will help you broaden your knowledge, such as band, orchestra, or choir. In addition, you should also take mathematics classes, since any musician needs to understand counting, rhythms, and beats. Many professional musicians write at least some of their own music, and a strong math background is very helpful for this. If your high school offers courses in music history or appreciation, be sure to take these. If you are interested in working in the classical music field, you will most likely need a college degree to succeed in this area. Therefore, be sure to round out your high school education by taking other college preparatory classes. Finally, no matter what type of musician you want to be, you will need to devote much of your after-school time to your private study and practice of music.

Postsecondary Training

Scores of colleges and universities have excellent music schools, and there are numerous conservatories that offer degrees in music. Many schools have noted musicians on their staff, and music students often have the advantage of studying under a professor who has a distinguished career in music. By studying with someone like this, you will not only learn more about music and performance, but you will also begin to make valuable connections in the field. You should know that having talent and a high grade point average do not always ensure entry into the top music schools. Competition for positions is extremely tough. You will probably have to audition, and only the most talented are accepted.

College undergraduates in music school generally take courses in music theory, harmony, counterpoint, rhythm, melody, ear training, applied music, and music history. Courses in composing, arranging, and conducting are available in most comprehensive music schools. Students will also have to take courses such as English and psychology along with a regular academic program.

Certification or Licensing

Musicians who want to teach in state elementary and high schools must be state certified. To obtain a state certificate, musicians must satisfactorily complete a degree-granting course in music education at an institution of higher learning. About 600 institutions in the United States offer programs in music education that qualify students for state certificates. Music education programs include many of the same courses mentioned earlier for musicians in general. They also include education courses and supervised practice teaching. To teach in colleges and universities or in conservatories generally requires a graduate degree in music. Widely recognized musicians, however, sometimes receive positions in higher education without having obtained a degree.

The American Guild of Organists offers a number of voluntary, professional certifications to its members. Visit the Guild's website (www.agohq.org) for more information.

Other Requirements

Hard work and dedication are key factors in a musical career, but music is an art form, and like those who practice any of the fine arts, musicians will succeed according to the amount of musical talent they have. Those who have talent and are willing to make sacrifices to develop it are the ones most likely to succeed. How much talent and ability one has is always open to speculation and opinion, and it may take years of studying and practice before musicians can assess their own degree of limitation.

Professional musicians generally hold membership in the American Federation of Musicians (AFL-CIO), and concert soloists also hold membership in the American Guild of Musical Artists, Inc. (AFL-CIO). Singers can belong to a branch of Associated Actors and Artists of America (AFL-CIO). Music teachers in schools often hold membership in MENC: The National Association for Music Education (formerly Music Educators National Conference).

EXPLORING

Elementary schools, high schools, and institutions of higher education all present a number of options for musical training and performance, including choirs, ensembles, bands, and orchestras. You also may have chances to perform in school musicals and talent shows. Those involved with services at churches, synagogues, or other religious institutions have excellent opportunities for exploring their interest in music. If you can afford to, take private music lessons.

Besides learning more about music, you will most likely have the chance to play in recitals arranged by your teacher. You may also want to attend special summer camps or programs that focus on the field. Interlochen Center for the Arts, for example, offers summer camps for students from the elementary to the high school level. College, university, and conservatory students gain valuable performance experience by appearing in recitals and playing in bands, orchestras, and school shows. The more enterprising students in high school and in college form their own bands and begin earning money by playing while still in school.

It is important for you to take advantage of every opportunity to audition so that you become comfortable with this process. There are numerous community amateur and semiprofessional theater groups throughout the United States that produce musical plays and operettas, in which beginning musicians can gain playing experience.

EMPLOYERS

Most musicians work in large urban areas and are particularly drawn to the major recording centers, such as

Chicago, New York City, Los Angeles, Nashville, and Miami Beach. Most musicians find work in churches, temples, schools, clubs, restaurants, and cruise lines, at weddings, in opera and ballet productions, and on film, television, and radio. Religious organizations are the largest single source of work for musicians.

Full-time positions as a musician in a choir, symphony orchestra, or band are few and are held only by the most talented. Musicians who are versatile and willing to work hard will find a variety of opportunities available, but all musicians should understand that work is not likely to be steady or provide much security. Many musicians support themselves in another line of work while pursuing their musical careers on a part-time basis. Busy musicians often hire agents to find employers and negotiate contracts or conditions of employment.

STARTING OUT

Young musicians need to enter as many playing situations as they can in their school and community musical groups. They should audition as often as possible, because experience at auditioning is very important. Whenever possible, they should take part in seminars and internships offered by orchestras, colleges, and associations. The National Orchestral Association offers training programs for musicians who want a career in the orchestral field.

Musicians who want to perform with established groups, such as choirs and symphony orchestras, enter the field by auditioning. Recommendations from teachers and other musicians often help would-be musicians obtain the opportunity to audition. Concert and opera soloists are also required to audition.

Popular musicians often begin playing at low-paying social functions and at small clubs or restaurants. If people like their performances, they usually move on to bookings at larger rooms in better clubs. Continued success leads to a national reputation and possible recording contracts. Jazz musicians tend to operate in the same way, taking every opportunity to audition with established jazz musicians.

Music teachers enter the field by applying directly to schools. College and university placement offices often have listings of positions. Professional associations frequently list teaching openings in their newsletters and journals, as do newspapers. Music-oriented journals— such as the American Federation of Musicians' journal *International Musician*—are excellent sources to check for job listings.

ADVANCEMENT

Popular musicians, once they have become established with a band, advance by moving up to more famous bands or by taking leadership of their own group. Bands may advance from playing small clubs to larger halls and even stadiums and festivals. They may receive a recording contract; if their songs or recordings prove successful, they can command higher fees for their contracts. Symphony orchestra musicians advance by moving to the head of their section of the orchestra. They can also move up to a position such as assistant or associate conductor. Once instrumental musicians acquire a reputation as accomplished artists, they receive engagements that are of higher status and remuneration, and they may come into demand as soloists. As their reputations develop, both classical and popular musicians may receive attractive offers to make recordings and personal appearances.

Popular and opera singers move up to better and more lucrative jobs through recognition of their talent by the public or by music producers and directors and agents. Their advancement is directly related to the demand for their talent and their ability to promote themselves.

Music teachers in elementary and secondary schools may, with further training, aspire to careers as supervisors of music of a school system, a school district, or an entire state. With further graduate training, teachers can qualify for positions in colleges, universities, and music conservatories, where they can advance to become department heads.

Well-known musicians can become artists-in-residence in the music departments of institutions of higher learning.

EARNINGS

It is difficult to estimate the earnings of the average musician, because what a musician earns is dependent upon his or her skill, reputation, geographic location, type of music, and number of engagements per year.

According to the American Federation of Musicians, musicians in the major U.S. symphony orchestras earned salaries of between $24,720 and $100,196 during the 2000–01 performance season. The season for these major orchestras, generally located in the largest U.S. cities, ranges from 24 to 52 weeks. Featured musicians and soloists can earn much more, especially those with an international reputation. According to the *Occupational Outlook Handbook,* median annual earnings of musicians, singers, and related workers were $36,740 in 2000.

Popular musicians are usually paid per concert or gig. A band just starting out playing a small bar or club may be required to play three sets a night, and each musician may receive next to nothing for the entire evening. Often bands receive a percentage of the cover charge at the door. Some musicians play for drinks alone. On average, however, pay per musician ranges from $30 to $300 or more per night. Bands that have gained recognition and a following may earn far more, because a club owner can usually be assured that many people will come to see the band play. The most successful popular musicians, of course, can earn millions of dollars each year. By the end of the 1990s, some artists, in fact, had signed recording contracts worth $20 million or more.

Musicians are well paid for studio recording work, when they can get it. For recording film and television background music, musicians are paid a minimum of about $185 for a three-hour session; for record company recordings they receive a minimum of about $235 for three hours. Instrumentalists performing live earn anywhere from $30 to $300 per engagement, depending on their degree of popularity, talent, and the size of the room they play.

According to the American Guild of Organists, full-time organists employed by religious institutions had the following base salary ranges by educational attainment in 2002: bachelor's degree, $35,285–$46,463; master's degree, $40,145–$53,610; and Ph.D., $45,225–$60,346.

The salaries received by music teachers in public elementary and secondary schools are the same as for other teachers. According to the U.S. Department of Labor, public elementary school and high school teachers had median yearly earnings of $41,820 in 1999–2000. Music teachers in colleges and universities have widely ranging salaries. Most teachers supplement their incomes through private instruction and by performing in their off hours.

Most musicians do not, as a rule, work steadily for one employer, and they often undergo long periods of unemployment between engagements. Because of these factors, few musicians can qualify for unemployment compensation. Unlike other workers, most musicians also do not enjoy such benefits as sick leave or paid vacations. Some musicians, on the other hand, who work under contractual agreements, do receive benefits, which usually have been negotiated by artists' unions, such as the American Federation of Musicians.

WORK ENVIRONMENT

Seldom are two days in a performer's life just alike. Musicians travel a great deal, thus their work conditions vary greatly. Performing musicians generally work in the evenings and on weekends. They also spend much time practicing and rehearsing for performances. Their workplace can be almost anywhere, from a swanky club to a high school gymnasium to a dark, dingy bar. Many concerts are given outdoors and in a variety of weather conditions. Performers may be given a star's dressing room, share a mirror in a church basement, or have to change in a bar's storeroom. They may work under the hot camera lights of film or television sets, or tour with a troupe in subzero temperatures. They may work amid the noise and confusion of a large rehearsal of a Broadway show, or in the relative peace and quiet of a small recording studio.

Music teachers affiliated with institutions work the same hours as other classroom teachers. Many of these teachers, however, spend time after school and on weekends directing and instructing school vocal and instrumental groups. Teachers may also have varied working conditions. They may teach in a large urban school, conducting five different choruses each day, or they may work in several rural elementary schools and spend much time driving from school to school.

College or university instructors may divide their time between group and individual instruction. They may teach several musical subjects and may be involved with planning and producing school musical events. They may also supervise student music teachers when they do their practice teaching.

Private music teachers work part or full time out of their own homes or in separate studios. The ambience of their workplace would be in accordance with the size and nature of their clientele.

OUTLOOK

It is difficult to make a living solely as a musician, and this will continue because competition for jobs will be as intense as it has been in the past. Most musicians must hold down other jobs while pursuing their music careers. Thousands of musicians are all trying to make it in the music industry. Musicians are advised to be as versatile as possible, playing various kinds of music and more than one instrument. More important, they must be committed to pursuing their craft.

The U.S. Department of Labor predicts that employment of musicians will grow about as fast as the average through 2010. The demand for musicians will be greatest in theaters, bands, and restaurants as the public continues to spend more money on recreational activities. The outlook is favorable in churches and other religious organizations. The increasing numbers of cable television networks and new television programs will likely cause an increase in employment for musicians. The number of record companies has grown dramatically over the last decade, particularly among small, independent houses. Digital recording technology has also made it easier and less expensive for musicians to produce and distribute their own recordings. However, few musicians will earn substantial incomes from these efforts. Popular musicians may receive many short-term engagements in nightclubs, restaurants, and theaters, but these engagements offer little job stability. The supply of musicians for virtually all types of music will continue to exceed the demand for the foreseeable future.

The opportunities for careers in teaching music are expected to grow at an average rate in elementary schools and in colleges and universities but at a slower rate in secondary schools. Although increasing numbers of colleges and universities are offering music programs, enrollments in schools at all levels have been depressed and are not expected to increase immediately in the next century. Some public schools facing severe budget problems have eliminated music programs altogether, making competition for jobs at that level even keener. In addition, private music teachers are facing greater competition from instrumental musicians who increasingly must turn to teaching because of the oversupply of musicians seeking playing jobs. Job availability is also diminishing because of the advent of electronic instruments such as synthesizers, which can replace a whole band, and the increasing trend to use recorded music.

TO LEARN MORE ABOUT MUSICIANS

BOOKS

Bruser, Madeline. *The Art of Practicing: A Guide to Making Music from the Heart.* New York: Bell Tower, 1999.

Field, Shelly. *Career Opportunities in the Music Industry.* New York: Facts On File, 2000.

Harnum, Jonathan. *Basic Music Theory: How to Read, Write, and Understand Written Music.* Fairbanks, Alaska: Questions, Ink: 2001.

McElerhan, Brock, and Lukas Foss. *Conducting Techniques for Beginners and Professionals.* New York: Oxford University Press, 1989.

Passman, Donald. *All You Need to Know About the Music Industry: Revised and Updated for the 21st Century.* New York: Simon & Schuster, 2000.

WEBSITES

American Guild of Musical Artists (AGMA)

www.musicalartists.org

The AGMA is a union for professional musicians. The website has information on upcoming auditions, news announcements for the field, and membership information.

Interlochen Center for the Arts

www.interlochen.org

The Interlochen Center provides information on summer camps for the arts.

MENC: The National Association for Music Education

www.menc.org

This organization supports public outreach programs, promotes music education, and offers information on the career of music teacher.

Music Teachers National Association (MTNA)

www.mtna.org

MTNA provides information on competitions for music students.

National Association of Schools of Music (NASM)

www.arts-accredit.org/nasm

NASM is an organization of schools, colleges, and universities that provide music education. Visit the website for a listing of NASM-accredited institutions.

WHERE TO WRITE

American Guild of Musical Artists (AGMA)
1430 Broadway, 14th Floor
New York, NY 10018
212-265-3687

MENC: The National Association for Music Education
1806 Robert Fulton Drive
Reston, VA 20191
800-336-3768

Music Teachers National Association
441 Vine Street, Suite 505
Cincinnati, OH 45202-2811
888-512-5278

National Association of Schools of Music (NASM)
11250 Roger Bacon Drive, Suite 21
Reston, VA 20190
703-437-0700

TO LEARN MORE ABOUT CONDOLEEZZA RICE

BOOKS

Dallin, Alexander, and Condoleezza Rice. *The Gorbachev Era*. Stanford, Calif.: Stanford Alumni Association, 1986.

Felix, Antonia. *Condi: The Condoleezza Rice Story*. New York: Newmarket Press, 2003.

Rice, Condoleezza. *The Soviet Union and the Czechoslovak Army, 1948-1983*. Princeton, N.J.: Princeton University Press, 1984.

Zelikow, Philip, and Condoleezza Rice. *Germany Unified and Europe Transformed: A Study in Statecraft*. Cambridge, Mass.: Harvard University Press, 1997.

WEBSITES

National Security Council
www.whitehouse.gov/nsc

Stanford University
www.stanford.edu

U.S. Department of State
www.state.gov

White House
www.whitehouse.gov

BIBLIOGRAPHY

BOOKS

Felix, Antonia. *Condi: The Condoleezza Rice Story.* New York: Newmarket Press, 2003.

The World Almanac and Book of Facts 2003. New York: World Almanac Books, 2003.

ARTICLES

"Bush's Foreign Policy Guru," *ABC News,* December 20, 2000.

"Condoleezza Rice: Rising Star," *BBC News,* December 18, 2000.

"Condoleezza Rice: National Security Adviser," *African Genesis,* December 2000–January 2001.

"Condoleezza Rice: The Devil's Handmaiden," *The Black Commentator,* January 23, 2003.

"New National Security Adviser of President-elect George W. Bush," *TIESWebzine,* June 2000.

"Powell: Blix Talks Termed 'Very Constructive,'" *CNN.com*, October 4, 2002.

"Powell's Key Points on Iraq," *CNN.com*, February 5, 2003.

"Search for Alliances, Criticism of '12,200-page Lie'", *CNN.com*, January 23, 2003.

"Situation Room Is White House's Nerve Center," *CNN.com*, April 2, 2003.

"U.S., UK Work on New Resolution," *CNN.com*, February 18, 2003.

Allen, Mike. "Rice: Race Can Be Factor in College Admissions," *Washington Post*, January 18, 2003.

Allen, Mike, and Charles Lane. "Rice Helped Shape Bush Decision on Admissions," *Washington Post*, January 17, 2003.

Bartels, Erin. "Condoleezza Rice's Chevron Service Could Pose Conflicts," *The Public i*, March 7, 2001.

Bock, Alan. "Scoping Out Condoleezza Rice," *Orange County Register*, December 27, 2000.

Bubnov, Vasily. "Will bin Laden Force Condoleezza Rice to Retire?", *PRAVDA*, May 20, 2002.

DeYoung, Karen, and Steven Mufson, "A Leaner and Less Visible NSC," *Washington Post*, February 10, 2001.

Eberhart, Dave. "MX Missile Retirement: Part of a Complex Shell Game," *NewsMax.com*, February 16, 2002.

Felix, Antonia. "Biography: Condoleezza Rice," transcript of interview, *Washington Post Live Online*, December 2, 2002.

Hawkins, B. Denise. "Condoleezza Rice's Secret Weapon," *Christian Reader*, September–October 2002.

Jackson, Bonita. "Fannie Lou Hamer: I'm Sick and Tired of Being Sick and Tired," *BeeJae's Little Piece of Cyberspace*, Minerva Computer Services, 1997.

Kettmann, Steve. "Bush's Secret Weapon," *Salon*, March 20, 2000.

Lehrer, Jim. Transcript of Newsmaker Interview with Condoleezza Rice, *Newshour* (Public Broadcasting Service), March 11, 2002.

Lemann, Nicholas. "Without a Doubt," *The New Yorker*, October 14 and 21, 2002.

Nimmo, Kurt. "What She <u>Really</u> Said: Condoleezza Rice at the Waldorf-Astoria," *Counterpunch*, October 10, 2002.

Noah, Timothy. "Whopper of the Week: Condoleezza Rice," *Slate*, May 23, 2002.

Oakes, Laurie. Transcript of interview with Condoleezza Rice, *ninemsn*, February 9, 2003.

Rice, Condoleezza. Transcript of speech at Republican National Convention, *Washington Post*, August 1, 2000.

Rice, Condoleezza. "Remarks on Terrorism and Foreign Policy," Paul H. Nitze School of Advanced International Studies, Johns Hopkins University, April 29, 2002 (released by Office of the Press Secretary, the White House).

Rice, Condoleezza. Transcript of press briefing, May 16, 2002 (released by press office, National Security Council).

Rice, Condoleezza. "Acknowledge That You Have an Obligation to Search for the Truth," *Stanford Report*, June 16, 2002.

Robinson, James. "Velvet-Glove Forcefulness," *Stanford Online Report*, June 9, 1999.

Sanger, David E., with John Tagliabue. "Bush Aide Says U.S., Not U.N., Will Rebuild Iraq," *New York Times*, April 5, 2003.

The White House. *The National Security Strategy of the United States of America*, September 17, 2002.

Warner, Margaret. Transcript of interview with Condoleezza Rice, *Newshour* (Public Broadcasting Service), September 25, 2002.

Wines, Michael. "Bush's Security Adviser Meets Putin in Effort to Repair War-Strained Relations," *New York Times*, April 8, 2003.

INDEX

ABOUT THE AUTHOR

Bernard Ryan Jr., has authored, coauthored, or ghost-written 29 books in many topics. Some of his books are *Tyler's Titanic,* a chapter book about the wreckage of the great ship on the ocean floor; *The Wright Brothers: Inventors of the Airplane,* which tells the Wrights' life stories and explains how they brought the world the miracle of flight; *Helping Your Child Start School,* an introduction to kindergarten for parents; *Simple Ways to Help Your Kids Become Dollar-Smart,* coauthored with financial planner Elizabeth Lewin; and *The Poisoned Life of Mrs. Maybrick,* the biography of the defendant in one of history's great murder trials. Mr. Ryan has written many shorter pieces for magazine and newspaper publication, and is a graduate of The Rectory School, Kent School, and Princeton University. He lives with his wife, Jean Bramwell Ryan, in Southbury, Connecticut. They have two daughters and two grandchildren.